digits™

PEARSON

Boston, Massachusetts • Chandler, Arizona • Glenview, Illinois • Upper Saddle River, New Jersey

Acknowledgments: Illustrations by Ralph Voltz and Laserwords

ISBN-13: 978-0-13-318094-7
ISBN-10: 0-13-318094-8
2 3 4 5 6 7 8 9 10 V011 15 14 13 12 11

digits™ System Requirements

▶ Supported System Configurations

	Operating System (32-bit only)	Web Browser* (32-bit only)	Java™ (JRE) Version**	JavaScript® Version***
PC	Windows® XP (SP3)	Internet Explorer® 7	Version 5.0, Update 11 or higher	1.4.2
	Windows Vista (SP1)	Internet Explorer 8	Version 5.0, Update 11 or higher	1.5
	Windows 7	Internet Explorer 9 (in compatibility mode)	Version 6.0, up to Update 18	1.6
Mac	Macintosh® OS 10.6	Safari® 5	Version 5.0, Update 16 or higher	1.5

* Pop-up blockers must be disabled in the browser.
** Java (JRE) plug-in must be installed.
*** JavaScript must be enabled in the browser.

▶ Additional Requirements

Software	Version
Adobe® Flash®	Version 10.1 or higher
Adobe Reader® (required for PC*)	Version 8 or higher
Word processing software	Microsoft® Word®, Open Office, or similar application to open ".doc" files

* Macintosh® OS 10.6 has a built-in PDF reader, Preview.

Screen Resolution
Minimum: 1024 x 768*
Maximum: 1280 x 1024
*recommended for interactive whiteboards

Internet Connection
Broadband (cable/DSL) or greater
is recommended.

Firefox Users
You cannot use the Firefox browser to
log in or view courses.

AOL® and AT&T™ Yahoo!® Users
You cannot use the AOL or AT&T Yahoo!
browsers. However, you can use AOL or
AT&T as your Internet Service Provider to
access the Internet, and then open a
supported browser.

▶ For *digits*™ Support

go to **http://support.pearsonschool.com/index.cfm/digits**

digits™ Learning Team

My Name: _____

My Teacher's Name: _____

My School: _____

Kala

Xiao

Lisa

Jay

Francis (Skip) Fennell
digits Author

Approaches to mathematics content and curriculum, educational policy, and support for intervention

Eric Milou
digits Author

Approaches to mathematical content and the use of technology in middle grades classrooms

Art Johnson
digits Author

Approaches to mathematical content and support for English language learners

William F. Tate
digits Author

Approaches to intervention, and use of efficacy and research

Helene Sherman
digits Author

Teacher education and support for struggling students

Grant Wiggins
digits Consulting Author

Understanding by Design

Stuart J. Murphy
digits Author

Visual learning and student engagement

Randall I. Charles
digits Advisor

Janie Schielack
digits Author

Approaches to mathematical content, building problem solvers, and support for intervention

Jim Cummins
digits Advisor

Supporting English Language Learners

Jacquie Moen
digits Advisor

Digital Technology

Log into **MyMathUniverse**

Be sure to save all of your your log-in information by writing it here.

Class URL: _____

My Username: _____

My Password: _____

1 First, go to MyMathUniverse.com.

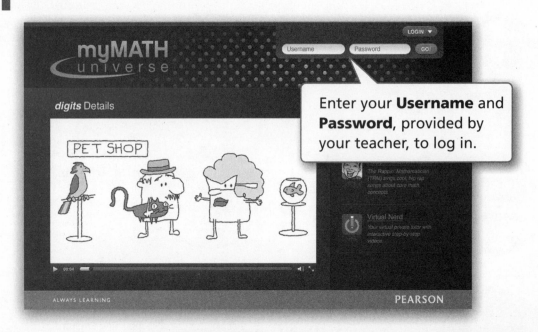

Enter your **Username** and **Password**, provided by your teacher, to log in.

2 After you've logged in, choose your class from the **home page.**

Choose **your class** from the list.

3 When you have chosen your class, this is your **Overview page.**

Click **To Do** to view your due items.

Click **Practice** to explore *digits* lessons on your own.

Click **Done** to view your past due and completed items.

Under **More** you can link to your **Grades** and **Reports**.

Click the **Calendar** to view items due each day. Red alarm clocks are for past due assignments!

Check your **Notifications**, including:
• Teacher Comments
• Grades posted
• Messages from your teacher
• Your progress in *digits*

As you work online, make sure to hit "Save" so you don't lose your work!

Save

Contents

Welcome to digits™

Using the Student Companion

digits is designed to help you master mathematics skills and concepts in a way that's relevant to you. As the title ***digits*** suggests, this program takes a digital approach. The Student Companion supports your work on ***digits*** by providing a place to demonstrate your understanding of lesson skills and concepts in writing.

Your companion supports your work on ***digits*** in so many ways!

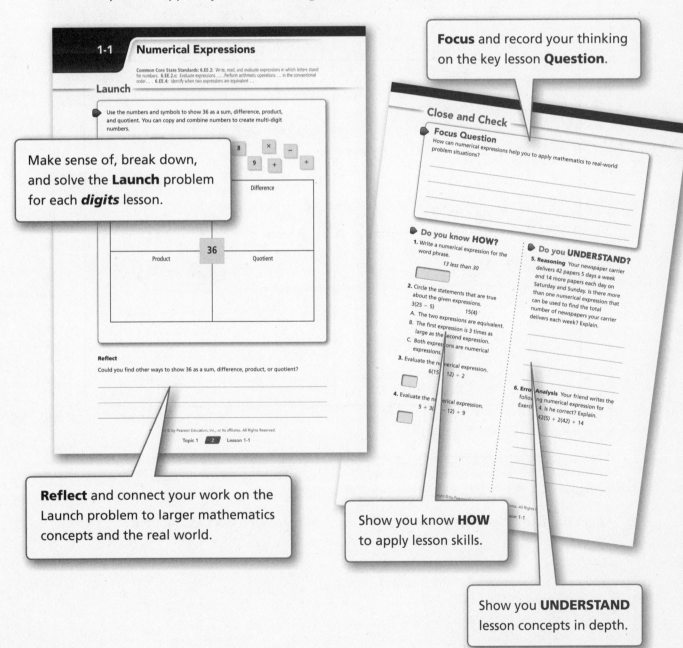

Focus and record your thinking on the key lesson **Question**.

Make sense of, break down, and solve the **Launch** problem for each ***digits*** lesson.

Reflect and connect your work on the Launch problem to larger mathematics concepts and the real world.

Show you know **HOW** to apply lesson skills.

Show you **UNDERSTAND** lesson concepts in depth.

Numerical Expressions

Common Core State Standards: 6.EE.2: Write, read, and evaluate expressions in which letters stand for numbers. 6.EE.2.c: Evaluate expressions ... . Perform arithmetic operations ... in the conventional order.... 6.EE.4: Identify when two expressions are equivalent ... .

Launch

Use the numbers and symbols to show 36 as a sum, difference, product, and quotient. You can copy and combine numbers to create multi-digit numbers.

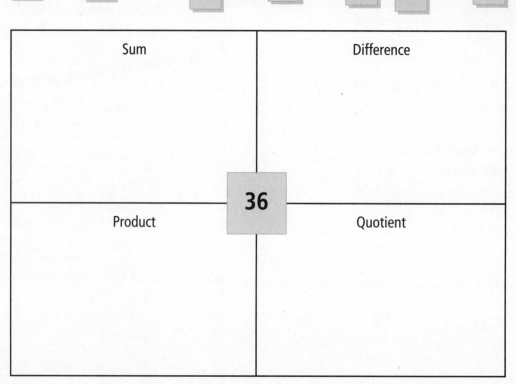

Reflect

Could you find other ways to show 36 as a sum, difference, product, or quotient?

_____

_____

_____

Close and Check

Topic 1 · 3 · Lesson 1-1

Focus Question

How can numerical expressions help you to apply mathematics to real-world problem situations?

_____

_____

_____

_____

▶ Do you know **HOW?**

1. Write a numerical expression for the word phrase.

13 less than 30

2. Circle the statements that are true about the given expressions.

$3(25 - 5)$ $15(4)$

A. The two expressions are equivalent.

B. The first expression is 3 times as large as the second expression.

C. Both expressions are numerical expressions.

3. Evaluate the numerical expression.

$6(15 - 12) \div 2$

4. Evaluate the numerical expression.

$5 + 3(42 - 12) \div 9$

▶ Do you **UNDERSTAND?**

5. Reasoning Your newspaper carrier delivers 42 papers 5 days a week and 14 more papers each day on Saturday and Sunday. Is there more than one numerical expression that can be used to find the total number of newspapers your carrier delivers each week? Explain.

_____

_____

_____

_____

6. Error Analysis Your friend writes the following numerical expression for Exercise 4. Is he correct? Explain.

$42(5) + 2(42) + 14$

_____

_____

_____

_____

Algebraic Expressions

Common Core State Standards: 6.EE.2.a: Write expressions ... with numbers and with letters standing for numbers ... . **6.EE.2.b:** Identify parts of an expression using mathematical terms ... . **6.EE.6:** Use variables to ... write expressions when solving a real-world ... problem ... . Also, **6.EE.2.**

Launch

Sort the five tiles into two groups. Describe each group.

Then, sort the five tiles into two groups again but in a different way. Describe each group.

| $a + 2$ | $9 - 2$ | 4×5 | $6 + y$ | $3 + 2$ |

Way 1

Group 1	Group 2

Way 2

Group 1	Group 2

Reflect

What could the letters a and y mean?

Close and Check

Focus Question

What does a variable allow you to do that you couldn't do before?

_____

_____

_____

_____

Do you know HOW?

1. Circle the algebraic expressions. Underline the numerical expressions.

   $9 + (15 - 7)$ $10c - 4$

   $14(13 - d)$ $6 \div (r + 2)$

2. You walk dogs in your neighborhood. You charge \$5 for each dog you walk. Sometimes you walk more than one dog a day. Sometimes you walk the same dog several days a week. Circle the variable quantities.

   A. The number of dogs you walk each day.

   B. The amount you charge for each dog.

   C. The number of times you walk each dog every week.

3. Which part of the expression represents a quotient of two terms?

   $3(4d - 8) + (7 - d) \div 5$

   [ ]

Do you UNDERSTAND?

4. **Vocabulary** What makes a constant term different from a term with a variable?

   _____

   _____

   _____

   _____

   _____

5. **Reasoning** To convert a temperature from degrees Celsius C to degrees Fahrenheit F, you can use the formula $F = C\left(\frac{9}{5}\right) + 32$. How do variables make this formula useful?

   _____

   _____

   _____

   _____

   _____

   _____

Writing Algebraic Expressions

Common Core State Standards: 6.EE.2: Write, read, and evaluate expressions in which letters stand for numbers. **6.EE.6:** Use variables to represent numbers and write expressions when solving a real-world or mathematical problem . . . . Also, **6.EE.2.a.**

Launch

 The city's second-best scientist invents a new and improved dog washing machine to sell to animal shelters. He charts the machine's performance.

How can he quickly figure out how many minutes it will take to wash any number of dogs? Use pictures, words, or symbols to tell how.

Dog Washing Machine Times

Dogs	Minutes to Wash
1	6
2	12
3	18
4	24
?	?

Reflect

Think about the pictures, words, or symbols you used. Which part represents what you know and which part represents what you don't know?

_____

_____

_____

Close and Check

Focus Question

Algebraic expressions allow you to describe situations where you don't know all of the information. How can you use algebraic expressions to help you make decisions?

_____

_____

_____

_____

Do you know HOW?

1. What is an algebraic expression for the product of 12 and a number?

2. You are 4 inches taller than your friend. Write an algebraic expression to represent how tall you are.

3. A satellite television provider charges $39.95 per month for service. On-demand movies can be rented for $3.99 each. Broadcasts of special events can be rented for $49.95 each. Write an algebraic expression to represent the total monthly cost if you rent m movies and s special events.

4. The movie shop sells posters for $7, DVDs for $15, and CDs for $9. Write an algebraic expression to represent the total cost for 2 posters, d DVDs, and c CDs.

Do you UNDERSTAND?

5. Writing Explain why two different variables, m and s, are needed in Exercise 3.

_____

_____

_____

_____

6. Reasoning How can the algebraic expression in Exercise 3 help you make a decision about how many on-demand movies and special events you can rent?

_____

_____

_____

_____

Evaluating Algebraic Expressions

Common Core State Standards: 6.EE.2: … evaluate expressions in which letters stand for numbers.
6.EE.2.c: Evaluate expressions at specific values of their variables. Include expressions that arise from formulas used in real-world problems … .

Launch

Your friend collects antique transit tokens. He likes to imagine what it was like to ride different buses and trains around the world. He records the value of each token in different ways.

Tell what you need to know to find the value of each token.

Token 1	**Token 2**

$45 \div 3$	$12 \times g$

Reflect

Which token could have any value based on the expression attached to it? Explain.

_____

_____

_____

_____

Close and Check

Focus Question

Algebraic expressions allow you to describe situations where you don't know all of the information. How can you use algebraic expressions to help you make decisions?

_____

_____

_____

_____

Do you know HOW?

1. Evaluate $117 - 5r$ for $r = 9$.

2. Evaluate $12x - (4y + 7z)$ for $x = 9$, $y = 4$, and $z = 2$.

3. Admission to an amusement park costs $35 for children, $52 for adults, and $29 for senior citizens. Write an expression to represent the cost of admission for any number of people.

4. Which would be less expensive: admission for 3 children and 3 senior citizens to the amusement park, or admission for 2 children and 3 adults? Write and evaluate the expression for the less expensive admission price.

Do you UNDERSTAND?

5. Error Analysis Your friend wrote an algebraic expression using only one variable for Exercise 3. Why is this incorrect?

_____

_____

_____

_____

_____

_____

6. Vocabulary What does it mean to evaluate an algebraic expression?

_____

_____

_____

_____

_____

Common Core State Standards: 6.EE.1: Write and evaluate numerical expressions involving whole-number exponents. **6.EE.2.c:** Evaluate expressions at specific values of their variables. Include expressions that arise from formulas used in real-world problems … .

Launch

Solve the riddle.

On day 1, you get 3 coins.
For each of the next 3 days,
your number of coins triples.
Write a numerical expression to show the
number of coins you will have in the end.
Then write the total number of coins.

Reflect

Suppose the tripling continues for 100 days. How would the numerical expression change? Explain.

_____

_____

_____

Close and Check

How do exponents allow you to communicate more precisely to others?

_____

_____

_____

_____

Do you know HOW?

1. What is the value of $6^3 - 100$?

2. What is the value of $5x^3 + 4y^3$ for $x = 4$ and $y = 3$?

3. A storage company uses boxes that have the same length, width, and height. Write and simplify an expression to show how much a box with side lengths that measure 4 ft can hold.

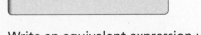

4. Write an equivalent expression using exponents.

$a \cdot 2 \cdot b \cdot a + b \cdot 2 \cdot a \cdot 2 \cdot b \cdot a$

Do you UNDERSTAND?

5. Writing You earn an allowance for chores you finish each week. You earn $2 on Monday. For the next 6 days, your daily earnings are twice what you earned the day before. Is this a reasonable weekly allowance? Explain.

_____

_____

_____

_____

6. Vocabulary You write an expression using exponents to show 4 multiplied by itself 6 times. Which number is the base and which number is the exponent? Explain.

_____

_____

_____

_____

Problem Solving

Common Core State Standards: 6.EE.2: Write, read, and evaluate expressions in which letters stand for numbers. **6.EE.2.a:** Write expressions that record operations with numbers and with letters standing for numbers . . . .

Launch

Pick one of the situations modeled below. Write an algebraic expression for it and tell how it matches the picture.

Algebraic Expression: [   ]

What It Means:

Reflect

What makes the situation you describe an algebraic expression instead of a numerical expression?

_____

_____

_____

_____

Close and Check

Focus Question

Algebraic expressions allow you to describe situations where you don't know all of the information. How can you use algebraic expressions to help you analyze relationships and simplify complicated situations?

_____

_____

_____

_____

Do you know HOW?

1. There are 432 students attending North Middle School. s number of them are sixth graders. Complete the bar diagram to model the expression for the number of students that are not sixth graders.

2. Boxes of fruit are delivered to a market. Each box holds 36 pieces of fruit. There are b number of boxes delivered each week. Complete the bar diagram to model the expression representing the total number of pieces of fruit delivered each week.

Do you UNDERSTAND?

3. Writing How do you know whether the variable in a bar diagram for a multiplication or division word problem goes above the diagram or in a section below?

_____

_____

_____

_____

4. Error Analysis Your friend wants to raise $235 by washing cars. He uses a bar diagram to decide how much to charge for each car. What error did he make?

_____

_____

_____

_____

The Identity and Zero Properties

Common Core State Standards: 6.EE.2.c: Evaluate expressions at specific values of their variables. Include ... real-world problems .... **6.EE.3:** Apply the properties of operations to generate equivalent expressions .... **6.EE.4:** Identify when two expressions are equivalent ... .

Launch

Your friend eats c number of carrots each week. Each carrot has 0 grams of fat.

Write an expression to show how many grams of fat are in c number of carrots. Then evaluate the expression for three different numbers of carrots. Explain your results.

Reflect

How would the problem change if a carrot had 1 gram of fat? Explain.

_____

_____

_____

Close and Check

Do you know HOW?

1. Circle the statements that illustrate the Zero Property of Multiplication.

$0a = 0$ $0 + (3d) = 3d$

$(3b + 4c)0 = 0$ $(c \cdot 12) + 0 = 12c$

2. Circle the property or properties illustrated by the statement $0 + (3d) = 1(3d)$.

Zero Property of Multiplication

Identity Property of Addition

Identity Property of Multiplication

3. In a certain game, some moves earn 3 points, some earn 1 point, and others earn 0 points. Use the expression $3e + 1c + 0i$ to find the total points scored by Player A.

Game Moves

	e	c	i
Player A	5	3	8
Player B	7	2	3

 points

Do you UNDERSTAND?

4. Reasoning In Exercise 3, did the player who made more moves score the most points? Explain. Use the Zero Property of Multiplication in your answer.

_____

_____

_____

_____

_____

5. Compare and Contrast How are the Identity Properties of Multiplication and Addition alike? How are they different?

_____

_____

_____

_____

_____

The Commutative Properties

Common Core State Standards: 6.EE.3: Apply the properties of operations to generate equivalent expressions .... **6.EE.4:** Identify when two expressions are equivalent (i.e., when the two expressions name the same number regardless of which value is substituted into them) .... .

Launch

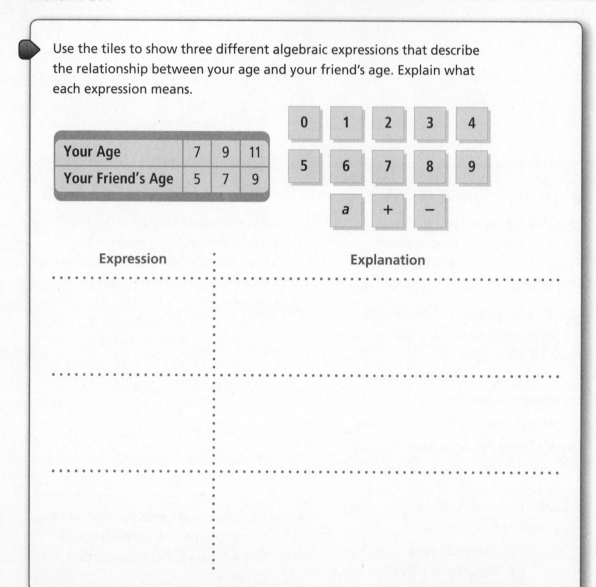

Use the tiles to show three different algebraic expressions that describe the relationship between your age and your friend's age. Explain what each expression means.

Your Age	7	9	11
Your Friend's Age	5	7	9

Tiles: 0 1 2 3 4 5 6 7 8 9 a + −

Expression	Explanation

Reflect

Was it easy or hard to think of three different expressions about the ages of you and your friend? Explain.

Close and Check

Focus Question

How can you apply what you know about the Commutative Properties in arithmetic to algebraic expressions?

_____

_____

_____

Do you know **HOW?**

1. Use the Commutative Property of Addition to write an expression equivalent to the one represented by the diagram.

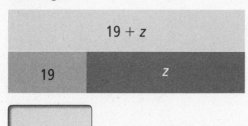

$19 + z$	
19	z

☐

2. A car gets 27 miles per gallon of gas. Write two equivalent expressions that show the total number of miles the car can travel on any number of gallons of gas.

☐ ☐

3. Draw lines to match the equivalent expressions in the two columns.

$7 + 2 + 9$ $8 \cdot 6 \cdot 3$

$1c \cdot 4r$ $ab + bc + cd$

$3 \cdot 6 \cdot 8$ $r \cdot 4 \cdot c$

$cb + dc + ba$ $9 + 2 + 7$

Do you **UNDERSTAND?**

4. Writing Clerk 1 uses the expression $4a + 3g - 2$ to find the total. Clerk 2 uses $3g + 4a - 2$. Will the totals be the same? Explain.

Apples: $4/bag
Grapes: $3/bag

Get $2 off today!

_____

_____

_____

5. Reasoning Can an equation show both the Identity Property of Addition and the Commutative Property of Addition? Explain.

_____

_____

_____

The Associative Properties

Common Core State Standards: 6.EE.3: Apply the properties of operations to generate equivalent expressions . . . . **6.EE.4:** Identify when two expressions are equivalent (i.e., when the two expressions name the same number regardless of which value is substituted into them) . . . .

Launch

Evaluate the expression $t + 89 + 11$, for $t = 38$. Show each step that you take.

Then evaluate the expression again for $t = 38$ but use different steps. Tell whether your first or second way was easier and explain why.

Way 1	Way 2
$t + 89 + 11$	$t + 89 + 11$

Reflect

Does it matter what steps you take when adding numbers?

_____

_____

_____

Close and Check

Focus Question

When can you regroup numbers? Why would you want to?

_____

_____

_____

_____

_____

Do you know HOW?

1. Use the Associative Property of Addition to write an expression equivalent to $(7 + 2) + t$.

2. There are 60 minutes in an hour and 24 hours in a day. How many minutes are in d days? Use the Associative Property of Multiplication to write two equivalent expressions.

3. Identify the property of addition or multiplication each expression models. Write **I** for Identity, **C** for Commutative, or **A** for Associative.

    $c + 8 + r = r + c + 8$

    $(wx) \cdot (yz) = w \cdot (xy) \cdot z$

    $abc = cba$

    $1c = c$

Do you UNDERSTAND?

4. Error Analysis Your friend uses the Associative Property to rewrite the expression $(6 \cdot 18) + 2$ as $6 \cdot (18 + 2)$ to make it easier to evaluate. Is he correct? Explain.

_____

_____

_____

_____

5. Reasoning Rewrite the expression using the Commutative and Associative Properties of Addition so that it can be evaluated using mental math. Then solve and explain your reasoning.

$$13 + 16 + 27 + 24$$

_____

_____

_____

_____

Greatest Common Factor

Common Core State Standards: 6.NS.4: Find the greatest common factor of two whole numbers less than or equal to 100 and the least common multiple of two whole numbers less than or equal to 12 ... .

Launch

A florist wants to use up all the flower shop's remaining roses and daisies to make several centerpieces. All the centerpieces need to be the same. What could each centerpiece look like? Describe the florist's options.

16 Roses

24 Daisies

Reflect

How did you determine if a centerpiece would match the florist's criteria?

_____

_____

_____

Close and Check

Focus Question

How does the greatest common factor relate two or more whole numbers?

_____

_____

_____

_____

Do you know **HOW?**

1. What is the greatest common factor of 64 and 72?

2. Write the prime factorization of 76.

3. Complete the factor trees below. Then use prime factorization to find the GCF of 45 and 60.

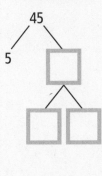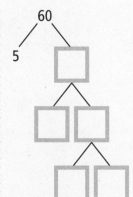

GCF:

Do you **UNDERSTAND?**

4. Writing To find the GCF of two numbers that have many factors, is it easier to list the factors of each number and compare or to find the prime factorization of each number and multiply common factors? Explain.

_____

_____

_____

_____

_____

5. Reasoning Do all composite numbers share a GCF that is greater than 1? Explain.

_____

_____

_____

_____

_____

The Distributive Property

Common Core State Standards: 6.NS.4: … Use the distributive property to express a sum of two whole numbers 1–100 with a common factor as a multiple of a sum of two whole numbers with no common factor … . **6.EE.3:** Apply the properties of operations to generate equivalent expressions … . Also, **6.EE.4.**

Launch

Three friends agree to paint parts of a background for a play. They know the width of each part but only agree that the height (*h*) of each part should be the same.

Write an expression for the area of each part. Then write an expression for the area of the whole background.

Area of
each part

Area of whole
background

Reflect

When they put the parts together, will the height of the background be *h* or 3 · *h*? Explain.

Close and Check

Focus Question

How does a common factor help you rewrite an expression? How does this help you think about a situation in a new way?

_____

_____

_____

_____

Do you know HOW?

1. Use the Distributive Property and GCF to write an expression equivalent to $24 - 18$.

2. Use the Distributive Property to write an expression equivalent to $7(2x^2 - 4x + 7)$.

3. Each day, a toy factory worker assembles 216 toys before his lunch break. After lunch, he assembles 168 more. Write 2 equivalent expressions to show how many toys the worker assembles in d days.

Do you UNDERSTAND?

4. **Compare and Contrast** You and a friend each rewrite the expression $45f - 24f$ using common factors. How are these expressions alike? How are they different?

$f(45 - 24)$ $3f(15 - 8)$

_____

_____

_____

_____

5. **Writing** Which of the three expressions in Exercise 4 do you think is the easiest to evaluate? Explain.

_____

_____

_____

_____

_____

Least Common Multiple

Common Core State Standards: 6.NS.4: Find the greatest common factor of two whole numbers less than or equal to 100 and the least common multiple of two whole numbers less than or equal to 12 ... .

Launch

A sports arena coordinator is scheduling games for November. The arena can host one game each day. So the coordinator schedules a basketball game every three days and a hockey game every four days. Will this schedule work? Explain your reasoning.

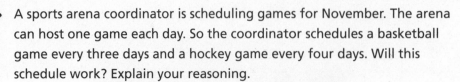

November						
Sun	Mon	Tues	Wed	Thurs	Fri	Sat
		1	2	3 B	4 H	5
6	7	8	9	10	11	12
13	14	15	16	17	18	19
20	21	22	23	24	25	26
27	28	29	30			

Reflect

Can you solve the problem without a calendar? Explain.

_____

_____

_____

_____

Close and Check

Focus Question

What does it mean for a number to be the least common multiple of two numbers?

_____

_____

_____

_____

Do you know **HOW?**

1. Find the least common multiple (LCM) of 6 and 8.

☐

2. Write and simplify an expression using the prime factorization of 16 and 20 to find the LCM.

☐

3. A page in a stamp album holds 18 stamps. A page in a photo album holds 8 photos. What is the least number of stamps and photos you need so that each album has the same number of items and only full pages?

☐

4. At a grand opening, every 15th customer to enter the bookstore receives a bookmark. Every 25th customer receives a $5 gift certificate. Which customer is the first to receive both gifts?

☐

Do you **UNDERSTAND?**

5. Reasoning A caterer orders table decorations for an event. One kind of decoration is sold in packs of 12. Another is sold in packs of 18. He finds the LCM before placing his order. Why might he have done this?

_____

_____

_____

_____

6. Compare and Contrast Explain what is the same about how you use prime factorization to find the greatest common factor and the least common multiple. What is different?

_____

_____

_____

_____

_____

Problem Solving

Common Core State Standards: 6.NS.4: Find the greatest common factor of two whole numbers less than or equal to 100 and the least common multiple of two whole numbers less than or equal to 12 ... .
6.EE.3: Apply the properties of operations to generate equivalent expressions ... .

Launch

Use the symbols, numbers, and variable to create three equivalent expressions. Tell which of the Topic's properties (Zero, Identity, Commutative, Associative, and Distributive) you use to create the expressions. You can use multiple copies of each tile if you wish.

( ) · + 2 3 6 s

Reflect

Can you model an expression using the Identity Property in this problem? Why or why not?

_____

_____

_____

Close and Check

Focus Question

How do the properties of operations help you solve problems?

_____

_____

_____

_____

Do you know HOW?

1. You have 33 party invitations to deliver. When you meet your friend, you have delivered 27 invitations. Your friend gives you 13 more to deliver. Use the Distributive Property to complete the equation to find how many invitations you still have to deliver.

3(⬜ − ⬜) + 13 = ⬜

2. A jewelry kit contains 126 beads and 96 charms. What is the greatest number of identical necklaces that can be made using all of the beads and charms?

3. Rewrite the expression using the Distributive Property.

$$21d + 27d + 15d$$

⬜

Do you UNDERSTAND?

4. Error Analysis Your friend tries to simplify the following expression but incorrectly applies a property. Explain his error and write the correct expression.

$$7 \cdot (6 - 3) = (7 - 6) \cdot (7 - 3)$$

_____

_____

_____

_____

_____

5. Reasoning One dog goes to the dog park every 6 days. Another dog goes to the park every 9 days. Today, both dogs are at the park. Should you use the GCF or LCM to find when both dogs will be at the park together again? Explain.

_____

_____

_____

Expressions to Equations

Common Core State Standards: 6.EE.2: Write, read, and evaluate expressions in which letters stand for numbers. **6.EE.5:** ... Use substitution to determine whether a given number in a specified set makes an equation or inequality true.

Launch

Shuffle the expressions in the top row of scales so that all of the scales in the bottom row balance.

This scale is balanced.

$7 + 9$

$2 \cdot 9$ $a + 11$ $4 \cdot 4$

$26 - 8$ $64 \div 4$

Reflect

What does it mean for two sides of the scale to be balanced?

_____

_____

_____

Close and Check

Focus Question

What is an equation? How is an equation with variables different from the equations you've seen in the past?

_____

_____

_____

Do you know HOW?

1. Complete the equation.

$$x(17 - 8) = \boxed{}\, x - 8\, \boxed{}$$

2. Match each expression with an equivalent expression.

A. $\frac{18w}{6}$ $\boxed{}$ $7w + 8w$

B. $20w + 12w$ $\boxed{}$ $10w \cdot 2$

C. $10w + 10w$ $\boxed{}$ $4w(5 + 3)$

D. $10w + 5w$ $\boxed{}$ $50w - 25w$

E. $25(2w - w)$ $\boxed{}$ $18w \div 6$

3. Circle the equations for which 5 is a solution.

$3x = 15$

$12 - a = 6$

$35 \div 7 = r$

$f + 9 = 14$

Do you UNDERSTAND?

4. Vocabulary Tell which of the following is an *expression* and which is an *equation*. Explain.

$$4t = 28 \qquad\qquad 8c + 7$$

_____

_____

_____

_____

_____

5. Error Analysis Your friend applied the Distributive Property to conclude that $8(x + 2)$ is equivalent to $8x + 2$. Describe your friend's error and give an expression that is equivalent.

_____

_____

_____

_____

_____

_____

_____

Common Core State Standards: 6.EE.2: Write, read, and evaluate expressions in which letters stand for numbers.

Launch

This scale is balanced. How could you keep the scale balanced if the left side changes to Box X and 5 pennies?

Reflect

How can you change the sides of a balanced scale and keep it balanced?

_____

_____

_____

Close and Check

Focus Question

How is it possible for two different equations to describe the same situation?
What does it mean for two equations to be equivalent?

_____

_____

_____

_____

▶ Do you know HOW?

1. A scale is balanced with 3a on one side and 9 on the other. What must you do to keep the scale balanced?

$$3a - 5 = 9 - \boxed{}$$

2. Use the information on the scale to complete the equivalent equation.

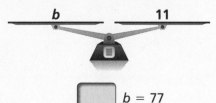

$$\boxed{} \; b = 77$$

3. Which equation is equivalent to $5c + 2 = 12$?

I. $5c + 2 = 12 + 2$

II. $5c + 2 - c = 12 - c$

III. $2(5c + 2) = 2(12)$

A. I and II

B. I and III

C. II and III

D. all of them

▶ Do you UNDERSTAND?

4. Reasoning Why is it important to do the same thing to both sides when balancing an equation?

_____

_____

_____

_____

_____

5. Error Analysis Describe and correct the error in writing an equivalent equation.

$$r + 6 = 16$$
$$r + 6 - 5 = 16 + 5$$

_____

_____

_____

_____

_____

Solving Addition and Subtraction Equations

Common Core State Standards: 6.EE.7: Solve real-world and mathematical problems by writing and solving equations of the form $x + p = q$ and $px = q$ for cases in which p, q and x are all nonnegative rational numbers.

Launch

Each row, column, and diagonal in the number square has the same sum.

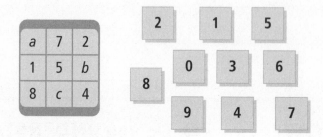

a	7	2
1	5	b
8	c	4

Find the values of a, b, and c.

$a = \boxed{}$ $b = \boxed{}$ $c = \boxed{}$

Explain.

Reflect

Did you use addition or subtraction to find each missing value? Could you use either operation?

_____

_____

_____

Close and Check

Focus Question

How do you use addition and subtraction to *undo* each other? Why might this be helpful in balancing equations?

_____

_____

_____

Do you know HOW?

1. Solve the equation.

$$7 + w = 23$$

$$w = \boxed{}$$

2. Write the inverse operation for each equation shown in the table below. Use **S** for subtraction and **A** for addition.

Equation	Inverse Operation
$12 + r = 47$	
$d - 15 = 4$	
$14 - s = 10$	
$t + 7 = 23$	
$56 + w = 92$	
$y - 8 = 61$	

3. Circle the equation that has a solution of 16.

$$x + 6 = 22 \qquad x - 6 = 22$$

Do you UNDERSTAND?

4. Vocabulary What are inverse operations? Give an example.

_____

_____

_____

_____

_____

5. Error Analysis Identify the error in solving the equation and give the correct answer.

$$5 + 7 + z = 33$$
$$12 + z = 33$$
$$12 + 12 + z = 33 + 12$$
$$z = 45$$

_____

_____

_____

_____

_____

Solving Multiplication and Division Equations

Common Core State Standards: 6.EE.7: Solve real-world and mathematical problems by writing and solving equations of the form $x + p = q$ and $px = q$ for cases in which p, q and x are all nonnegative rational numbers.

Launch

Some students sign up for summer swim classes. The swim coach splits them evenly to form 13 classes with 8 students in each class. How many students sign up for swim class?

Show how to solve the problem using division and multiplication.

Division	Multiplication

Reflect

Could you have solved the problem using only division and not any multiplication? How?

_____

_____

_____

Close and Check

Focus Question

How do you use multiplication and division to *undo* each other? Why might this be helpful in balancing equations?

_____

_____

_____

▶ Do you know **HOW?**

1. Write and solve the modeled equation.

42						
x	x	x	x	x	x	x

$\boxed{}\, x = \boxed{}$

$x = \boxed{}$

2. Write the inverse operation for each equation shown in the table below. Use **A** for addition, **S** for subtraction, **M** for multiplication and **D** for division.

Equation	Inverse Operation
$36 = 12r$	
$d \div 15 = 4$	
$5 + f = 13$	
$56 = 7t$	
$14 \div s = 2$	
$63 - p = 46$	

▶ Do you **UNDERSTAND?**

4. Writing Draw and explain a model of the equation $3x = 18$.

_____

_____

_____

_____

_____

5. Reasoning A teacher has 72 pencils to split among 24 students. She asks the class to write an equation to figure out how many each gets.

Student A writes: $72 \div 24 = x$

Student B writes: $24x = 72$

Who is correct? Explain.

_____

_____

_____

Equations to Inequalities

Common Core State Standards: 6.EE.8: Write an inequality ... to represent a constraint or condition in a real-world or mathematical problem. Recognize that inequalities of the form $x > c$ or $x < c$ have infinitely many solutions; represent solutions of such inequalities on number line diagrams.

Launch

The long jump record at the local school is 18 feet. Describe a jump that could break the record in three different ways—using a picture, using words, and using symbols.

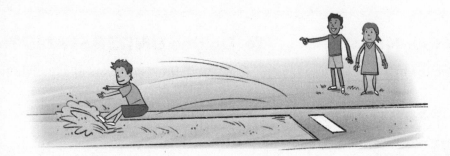

Picture	Words	Symbols

Reflect

How many jumps could tie the record? How many jumps could break the record?

_____

_____

_____

Close and Check

Focus Question

How does the concept of *inequality* help you describe situations?

_____

_____

_____

_____

Do you know HOW?

1. Tell whether each statement can be written as an equality or an inequality. Write **E** for equality and **I** for inequality.

Statement	Equality or Inequality
The temperature will reach at least 72° today.	
My puppy is six months old today.	
There are no more than 31 days in any given month.	
There are less than 28 students in each classroom.	
There are the same number of boys as there are girls in my family.	

2. Use the number line to graph the inequality.

$$x \leq 6$$

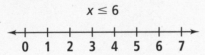

Do you UNDERSTAND?

3. Writing Which of the following graphs includes 4 in its solution set? Explain.

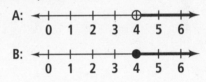

_____

_____

_____

4. Reasoning For safety, riders of an amusement park roller coaster must be at least 4 ft 6 in. tall. Write the inequality to show this. Then describe why an inequality represents this situation better than an equation.

_____

_____

_____

_____

_____

Solving Inequalities

Common Core State Standards: 6.EE.5: ... Use substitution to determine whether a given number in a specified set makes an equation or inequality true. **6.EE.8:** ... Recognize that inequalities of the form $x > c$ or $x < c$ have infinitely many solutions; represent solutions ... on number line diagrams.

Launch

You have $27 and want to invite the most friends possible to go to a concert. What is the greatest number of people, including you, that can go? Explain.

Reflect

Could fewer friends go with you to the concert?

_____

_____

_____

Close and Check

▶ Do you know HOW?

1. Circle the inequalities that have 25 as a solution.

$72 + x < 100$ $216 \geq 4x$ $x + 13 < 38$

$45 - x > 131$ $x \div 7 \leq 9$

2. Complete the steps to solve the inequality.

$$h \div 4 > 6$$

$$h \div 4 \cdot \boxed{} > 6 \cdot \boxed{}$$

$$h > \boxed{}$$

3. Graph the inequalities on the number lines.

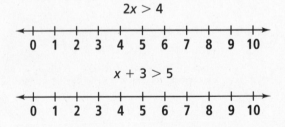

$2x > 4$

$x + 3 > 5$

▶ Do you UNDERSTAND?

4. Reasoning Are the inequalities in Exercise 3 equivalent? How do you know?

5. Error Analysis The following inequalities are displayed in your class.

$$y > 4 \qquad g < 8$$

Your classmate says that the inequalities are equivalent because 5 is a solution of both. Is she correct? Explain your reasoning.

Problem Solving

Common Core State Standards: **6.EE.7:** Solve real-world and mathematical problems by writing and solving equations of the form $x + p = q$ and $px = q$ for cases in which p, q and x are all nonnegative rational numbers. Also, **6.EE.5.**

Launch

Use the clues to find the value of each gemstone. Match the gemstone values to the lock numbers to open the treasure chest.

Reflect

How would the problem change if the clues had letters instead of shapes?

_____

_____

_____

_____

Close and Check

Do you know HOW?

1. A food bank needs donations of 1,275 cans of food each month. This month, 729 more cans of food are needed. How many cans of food have already been donated? Complete the model and write an equation to represent the problem.

2. A dragonfly can fly up to 7 meters per second. It travels 56 meters to catch a mosquito. What is the time t it takes the dragonfly to catch it? Write and solve an inequality to model the situation.

Do you UNDERSTAND?

3. Writing What clues can you use to determine whether a problem represents an equality or an inequality?

_____

_____

_____

_____

_____

4. Reasoning The inequality $x > 8$ is displayed on chart paper. Your teacher asks you to list all of the solutions to this inequality. Can you list all of the solutions? Explain why or why not.

_____

_____

_____

_____

_____

Using Two Variables to Represent a Relationship

Common Core Standards: 6.EE.9: Use variables to represent two quantities in a real-world problem that change in relationship to one another; write an equation to express one quantity ... in terms of the other quantity ... .

Launch

Think inside and outside the box. Inside the box, write three things that relate to the weight of the box. Outside the box, write three things about the box that do not relate to its weight.

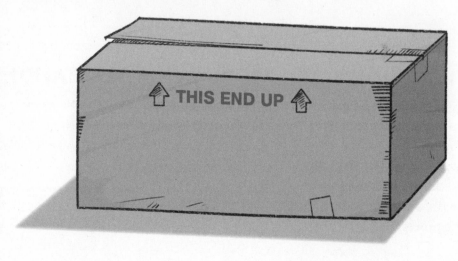

Reflect

Why does it matter what things relate to the weight of the box?

_____

_____

_____

Close and Check

Focus Question

What does it mean for one quantity to depend on another? How do you represent such a relationship?

_____

_____

_____

_____

Do you know HOW?

1. Circle the related and unknown quantities in the word problem.

> A conservation program plants 756 trees to reforest an area of land. A number of the trees are coniferous and a number of the trees are deciduous.

2. Write an equation to represent the situation above.

3. In each situation, underline the independent variable, and then circle the dependent variable.

A. The wind chill factor is related to the wind speed.

B. The amount of merchandise bought determines the amount of sales tax charged.

C. You earned d dollars for working h hours.

Do you UNDERSTAND?

4. Vocabulary How can you determine which variable is dependent and which variable is independent? Give an example.

_____

_____

_____

_____

5. Error Analysis A classmate writes an equation to determine how many boys b she can invite to her party after she invites her girlfriends g. She is allowed to have 25 guests. Explain her mistake, and then write the correct equation.

$$g - b = 25$$

_____

_____

_____

_____

Analyzing Patterns Using Tables and Graphs

Common Core Standards: 6.NS.8: Solve real-world and mathematical problems by graphing points in ... the coordinate plane ... . **6.EE.9:** ... Analyze the relationship between the dependent and independent variables using graphs and tables ... .

Launch

Each time you open a box, you see two more boxes. There are seven boxes in all.

What is the minimum number of boxes you need to open to see all seven boxes? Explain your reasoning.

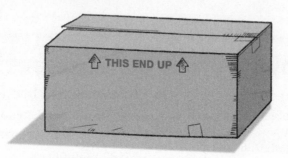

Reflect

What are the dependent and independent variables in the problem?

_____

_____

_____

_____

Close and Check

Focus Question

How do you find a pattern in a table?

_____

_____

_____

_____

Do you know HOW?

1. Toys are shipped to a store by the box. Determine the pattern and complete the table to show how many toys are delivered for each number of boxes shipped.

Boxes	0	2		
Toys	0	20		

2. Use the table above to graph the relationship between the number of boxes shipped and the number of toys delivered.

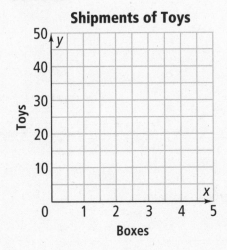

Shipments of Toys

Do you UNDERSTAND?

3. **Writing** The data for each 10-year census for the past 100 years is graphed. How can the graph be used to estimate the population between each census?

_____

_____

_____

_____

4. **Error Analysis** A classmate says the y column increases by 12 each time, so the next point (x, y) is (6, 42). Explain his mistake and tell what he should have written.

x	1	3	5	**6**
y	6	18	30	**42**

_____

_____

_____

_____

Relating Tables and Graphs to Equations

Common Core Standards: 6.EE.9: Use variables to represent two quantities in a real-world problem ... write an equation to express one quantity ... in terms of the other quantity ... Analyze the relationship between the variables using graphs and tables, and relate these to the equation.

Launch

Label each column in the table to reflect the pattern in the shapes. Then describe at least three patterns you see, within or across columns, using those label names.

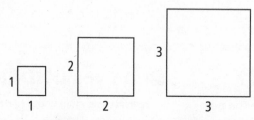

1	1	4
2	4	8
3	9	12

Pattern 1	Pattern 2	Pattern 3

Reflect

Where have you seen the patterns in this problem before? Explain.

Close and Check

Focus Question

How are graphs, tables, and equations related?

_____

_____

_____

_____

Do you know **HOW?**

1. Use the table to relate the independent variable x to the dependent variable y. Write an equation that shows the relationship.

x	y
3	12
5	14
7	16
9	18

2. Use the graph to write an equation that represents the relationship between x and y.

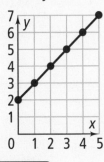

Do you **UNDERSTAND?**

3. Reasoning Is it easier to write an equation based on a graph or a table? Explain.

_____

_____

_____

_____

_____

4. Error Analysis A classmate says the graph in Exercise 2 could represent the number of tokens won at an arcade. Explain the error in her suggestion.

_____

_____

_____

_____

_____

Problem Solving

Common Core Standards: 6.EE.2.c: Evaluate expressions at specific values of their variables ... .
6.EE.9: Use variables to represent two quantities in a real-world problem ... write an equation to express
one quantity ... in terms of the other quantity ... .

Launch

Two friends need to save more money for a $300 trip. They decide to mow lawns. Each friend picks a different method to determine how many lawns they need to mow to save enough money.

Describe why each method works. Which method would you use? Explain your reasoning.

Method 1

Lawns Mowed	Future Savings
1	$23
2	$38
3	$53
4	$68

Method 2

$$T = 15\ell + 8$$

Reflect

How much money do the friends have before mowing lawns? Explain.

_____

_____

_____

Close and Check

Focus Question
What types of problems are best solved using tables?

_____

_____

_____

Do you know HOW?

1. You save the $50 you received for your birthday and $5 each week. Write an equation that relates the week w to the amount of money m saved.

[   ]

2. Three friends share a secret. Every day after that, the number of people who know the secret triples. Write an equation that relates the day d to the number of people p who know the secret.

[   ]

3. A job has 2 pay options. Option 1 pays $25 each day. Option 2 pays $2 the first day and doubles the amount for each day worked. Write an equation for each option that relates the days worked d to the total earned t.

Option 1   Option 2

[   ]   [   ]

Do you UNDERSTAND?

4. **Writing** Based on Exercise 3, how many days would you have to work to earn more in one day on Option 2 than you would in one day on Option 1? Explain how you made your decision.

_____

_____

_____

_____

_____

5. **Error Analysis** Every week there are 5 times as many fruit flies in a colony as the week before. The colony begins with 5 fruit flies. Your friend writes the equation $f = w^5$ to relate the week w to the number of flies f. Explain his mistake and write the correct equation.

_____

_____

_____

_____

Multiplying Fractions and Whole Numbers

Common Core Standards: 6.NS.1: Interpret and compute quotients of fractions, and solve word problems involving division of fractions by fractions, e.g., by using visual fraction models and equations to represent the problem.

Launch

Compare $\frac{1}{3} \cdot 5$ and $\frac{1}{5} \cdot 3$. Without finding the product of each expression, tell which expression has the greater product. Use pictures and words to support your argument.

Reflect

How many copies of a unit fraction like $\frac{1}{4}$ do you need to have a product equal to 1? Greater than 1? Explain.

_____

_____

_____

Close and Check

Focus Question

Is multiplying a whole number and a fraction different from multiplying a fraction and a whole number? Explain.

_____

_____

_____

_____

Do you know HOW?

1. Write the multiplication equation that matches the model.

2. Use the diagram to show $3 \cdot \frac{3}{4}$. Then write the product in simplest form.

[ ]

[ ]

[ ]

[ ]

3. Find the product of $\frac{5}{6} \cdot 7$ and write it in simplest form.

[ ]

Do you UNDERSTAND?

4. Error Analysis A student draws this diagram to model $2 \cdot \frac{1}{4}$. Describe the error and draw a correct model.

_____

_____

_____

5. Reasoning A recipe calls for $3\frac{3}{4}$ cups of berries. You need to make 5 batches of the recipe for a party. You have 18 cups of berries. Do you have enough berries? Explain.

_____

_____

_____

_____

Multiplying Two Fractions

Common Core Standards: 6.NS.1: Interpret and compute quotients of fractions, and solve word problems involving division of fractions by fractions, e.g., by using visual fraction models and equations to represent the problem.

Launch

Your favorite museum is $\frac{3}{4}$ mile from your home. You walk $\frac{1}{2}$ of the way there and ride the bus $\frac{1}{2}$ of the way there.

Tell how far you walk. Include a picture in your response.

Reflect

How can you find $\frac{1}{2}$ of a whole number like 1? Do you do something different to find $\frac{1}{2}$ of a fraction like $\frac{3}{4}$? Explain.

_____

_____

_____

Close and Check

Focus Question

Is the product of two proper fractions greater than the fractions being multiplied? Explain.

_____

_____

_____

_____

Do you know HOW?

1. Use the unit square to show $\frac{3}{4}$ of $\frac{1}{3}$. Write the product in simplest form.

2. Find the product of $\frac{7}{12} \cdot \frac{4}{5}$. Write the product in simplest form.

3. Find the area of the postage stamp in simplest form.

$\frac{5}{9}$ in.

$\frac{3}{10}$ in.

44

Do you UNDERSTAND?

4. Compare and Contrast How is the product of a proper fraction and a whole number similar to and different from the product of two proper fractions?

_____

_____

_____

_____

_____

_____

5. Reasoning How does predicting the range of the product help in problem solving?

_____

_____

_____

_____

Multiplying Fractions and Mixed Numbers

Common Core Standards: 6.NS.1: Interpret and compute quotients of fractions, and solve word problems involving division of fractions by fractions, e.g., by using visual fraction models and equations to represent the problem.

Launch

Your neighbor plans a rectangular garden 3 yards long by $3\frac{1}{2}$ yards wide.

What will the area of the garden be? Show how you found out.

3 yd

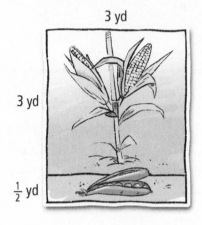

3 yd

$\frac{1}{2}$ yd

Reflect

Think about the different properties you studied in Topic 2: the Zero Property, Identity Properties, Commutative Properties, Distributive Property, and Associative Property. Explain how you could use one of the properties in this problem.

_____

_____

Close and Check

Focus Question

How can you compare the product of a proper fraction and a mixed number to the fraction? How can you compare the product of a proper fraction and a mixed number to the mixed number?

_____

_____

_____

▶ Do you know **HOW?**

1. A water cooler holds $4\frac{1}{2}$ gallons of water. The container is $\frac{2}{3}$ full. Use the grid to show how many gallons of water are in the cooler.

▢ gallons

2. A gas tank holds $9\frac{1}{2}$ gallons of gas. The tank is $\frac{8}{9}$ full. How many gallons of gas are in the tank?

 gallons

3. Find the area of the bookmark below.

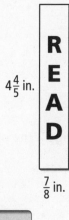

$4\frac{4}{5}$ in.

$\frac{7}{8}$ in.

▢

▶ Do you **UNDERSTAND?**

4. Reasoning Explain how you know that finding a fractional part of a whole number is the same as multiplying that fraction by a whole number.

_____

_____

_____

5. Compare and Contrast Show two ways to model $2\frac{1}{2} \cdot \frac{1}{2}$. Explain which way you prefer.

_____

_____

_____

Multiplying Mixed Numbers

Common Core Standards: 6.NS.1: Interpret and compute quotients of fractions, and solve word problems involving division of fractions by fractions, e.g., by using visual fraction models and equations to represent the problem.

Launch

Your neighbor's garden plan grows to include tomatoes and pumpkins. The garden is now $4\frac{1}{2}$ yd long and $3\frac{1}{2}$ yd wide. What is the area of the garden now? Show how you found out.

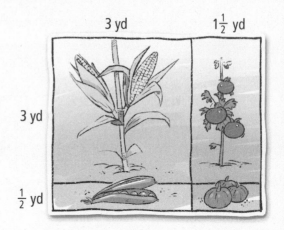

3 yd $1\frac{1}{2}$ yd

3 yd

$\frac{1}{2}$ yd

Reflect

Your neighbor plans a $4\frac{1}{2}$ yd by $3\frac{1}{2}$ yd garden. Would the area change if the plan changed to a $3\frac{1}{2}$ yd by $4\frac{1}{2}$ yd garden? Explain.

_____

_____

_____

Close and Check

Do you know HOW?

1. Write and solve an equation using mixed numbers to represent the model.

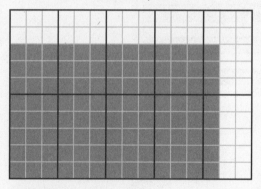

Do you UNDERSTAND?

4. Writing How might the Distributive Property make multiplying a whole number and a mixed number easier?

2. Find the area of the drawing.

$4\frac{1}{3}$ in.

$2\frac{3}{5}$ in.

3. Use the Distributive Property to rewrite the expression $5 \cdot 4\frac{11}{12}$.

5. Error Analysis Each sandwich uses $3\frac{7}{8}$ ounces of turkey. There is enough turkey for $4\frac{1}{2}$ sandwiches. You estimate that there is about 16 ounces of turkey. Your friend estimates the weight to be about 12 ounces. Which estimate is better? Explain.

Problem Solving

Common Core Standards: 6.NS.1: Interpret and compute quotients of fractions, and solve word problems involving division of fractions by fractions, e.g., by using visual fraction models and equations to represent the problem.

Launch

The length of a United States flag must be $1\frac{9}{10}$ times its width. A flag company plans a large flag with a width of $8\frac{1}{2}$ feet. What must the length be? Explain.

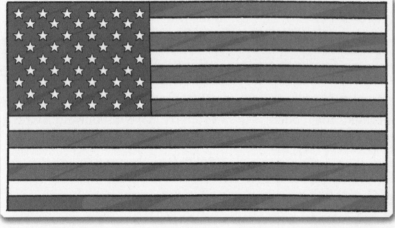

$8\frac{1}{2}$ ft

? ft

Reflect

You used estimation to check reasonableness when multiplying whole numbers. Can you do the same when multiplying mixed numbers? What would you estimate for this problem?

_____

_____

_____

Close and Check

Focus Question

What real-world problems can be solved by multiplying fractions or mixed numbers?

_____

_____

_____

_____

Do you know HOW?

1. Use $>$, $<$, or $=$ to compare each expression to the given fraction.

$3\frac{5}{6} \cdot 2\frac{1}{3}$ $3\frac{5}{6}$

$2\frac{4}{9} \cdot \frac{3}{3}$ $2\frac{4}{9}$

$1\frac{1}{10} \cdot \frac{1}{10}$ $1\frac{1}{10}$

2. A contractor needs $3\frac{3}{5}$ gallons of water for each batch of cement. How many gallons water will he need to make $9\frac{1}{2}$ batches of cement?

 gallons

3. On the first day, a bird feeder is $\frac{9}{10}$ full of seeds. Each following day, the feeder contains $\frac{2}{3}$ of the amount from the day before. How full will the bird feeder be on the fourth day?

Do you UNDERSTAND?

4. Reasoning How can multiplying fractions and mixed numbers be useful when making more or less than one full batch of the pretzel recipe?

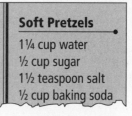

Soft Pretzels
1¼ cup water
½ cup sugar
1½ teaspoon salt
½ cup baking soda

_____

_____

_____

5. Writing Write a word problem that you could use the expression to solve.

$$2\frac{1}{2} \cdot 4\frac{1}{4}$$

_____

_____

_____

Dividing Fractions and Whole Numbers

Common Core Standards: 6.NS.1: Interpret and compute quotients of fractions, and solve word problems involving division of fractions by fractions, e.g., by using visual fraction models and equations to represent the problem.

Launch

Find each quotient. Use a picture to represent each problem.

$4 \div 4$

$4 \div 2$

$4 \div 1$

$4 \div \frac{1}{2}$

Reflect

Which problem resulted in a quotient greater than 4? Why do you think that happened?

_____

_____

_____

_____

Close and Check

Focus Question

How does the relationship between multiplication and division help you to divide fractions and whole numbers?

_____

_____

_____

_____

Do you know HOW?

1. Use the number line to model $\frac{4}{5} \div 2$. Then write the solution.

0   1

2. Circle the division equation modeled by the number line.

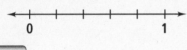

0   1   2   3   4

A. $3 \div \frac{1}{4}$

B. $12 \div \frac{1}{3}$

C. $4 \div \frac{1}{3}$

3. A fabric store donates 15 yards of fabric for a community quilt project. Each piece of fabric measures $\frac{5}{8}$ yard. How many $\frac{5}{8}$-yard pieces of fabric is the store donating?

Do you UNDERSTAND?

4. Reasoning Will the quotient of a proper fraction divided by a whole number ever result in a whole number? Explain.

_____

_____

_____

_____

_____

5. Writing Explain why the first expression can be rewritten as the second expression.

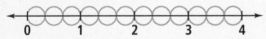
$$5 \div \frac{2}{3} \qquad 5 \cdot \frac{3}{2}$$

_____

_____

_____

_____

_____

Dividing Unit Fractions by Unit Fractions

Common Core Standards: 6.NS.1: Interpret and compute quotients of fractions, and solve word problems involving division of fractions by fractions, e.g., by using visual fraction models and equations to represent the problem.

Launch

A customer orders $\frac{1}{2}$ pound of tuna for a special treat for his cats. He asks the deli worker to divide the tuna into $\frac{1}{10}$-pound pieces so each cat gets the same treat.

How many cats does the customer have? Show how you know.

Reflect

Suppose the customer ordered 20 pounds of tuna and asked for it to be divided into 5-pound pieces. Would you have solved the problem differently working with whole numbers compared to working with unit fractions? Explain.

_____

_____

_____

Close and Check

Focus Question

Using models can help you divide unit fractions. Using reciprocals can also help you divide unit fractions. Which method is best in which situations?

_____

_____

_____

_____

▶ Do you know **HOW?**

1. Use the number line to model $\frac{1}{2} \div \frac{1}{10}$. Then write the solution.

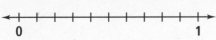

2. A community garden is being plotted on a $\frac{1}{60}$-square-mile site. The length of the garden is $\frac{1}{12}$ mile. How wide, in miles, is the garden plot?

 mile

3. How many $\frac{1}{21}$-yard pieces can be cut from a $\frac{1}{3}$-yard piece of string? Write and solve an equation.

4. A farmer needs to replace $\frac{3}{4}$ mi of fence. The first corner post does not need replaced. If he places a post every $\frac{1}{12}$ mi, how many fence posts will he need?

▶ Do you **UNDERSTAND?**

5. Writing How did you decide which fraction is the dividend and which fraction is the divisor in Exercise 3?

_____

_____

_____

_____

6. Error Analysis A man purchases $\frac{1}{2}$ pound of seeds to make bird feeders. Each feeder requires $\frac{1}{16}$ pound of seeds. He sets up an equation to find how many bird feeders he can make. Explain his error and find the number of feeders he can make.

$$\frac{1}{16} \div \frac{1}{2} = \frac{1}{8}$$

_____

_____

_____

_____

_____

Dividing Fractions by Fractions

Common Core Standards: 6.NS.1: Interpret and compute quotients of fractions, and solve word problems involving division of fractions by fractions, e.g., by using visual fraction models and equations to represent the problem.

Launch

Find the fraction that makes this number sentence true.
Explain how you know you are right.

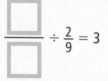

$$\frac{\square}{\square} \div \frac{2}{9} = 3$$

Reflect

How are multiplication and division related? Does it matter if the numbers involved are whole numbers or fractions?

_____

_____

_____

Close and Check

Do you know HOW?

1. One lap of a running track is $\frac{7}{8}$ mile. Each member of the relay team sprints $\frac{7}{16}$ mile before handing the baton to the next runner. Use the number line to find how many team members must run to complete one lap of the track.

 team members

2. Find $\frac{9}{11} \div \frac{3}{8}$. Simplify the quotient.

3. How many $\frac{3}{16}$-pound servings of fish there are in a package containing $\frac{9}{14}$ pound of fish? Write and solve an equation. Simplify the quotient.

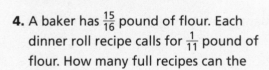

4. A baker has $\frac{15}{16}$ pound of flour. Each dinner roll recipe calls for $\frac{1}{11}$ pound of flour. How many full recipes can the baker make?

Do you UNDERSTAND?

5. **Writing** Write and solve a fraction story problem using the following expression: $\frac{11}{12} \div \frac{2}{9} = 4\frac{1}{8}$.

6. **Error Analysis** A classmate says $\frac{15}{16} \div \frac{3}{4} = \frac{3}{4} \div \frac{15}{16}$. Is your classmate correct? Explain.

Dividing Mixed Numbers

Common Core Standards: 6.NS.1: Interpret and compute quotients of fractions, and solve word problems involving division of fractions by fractions, e.g., by using visual fraction models and equations to represent the problem.

Launch

Without dividing, tell which expression will result in a quotient greater than $\frac{1}{2}$ and which will result in a quotient less than $\frac{1}{2}$. Explain how you know.

Expression 1

$\frac{1}{2} \div \frac{4}{3}$

Expression 2

$\frac{1}{2} \div \frac{3}{4}$

Expression 3

$\frac{1}{2} \div 1\frac{1}{4}$

Reflect

Does dividing by a fraction always result in a quotient greater than the dividend? Explain.

_____

_____

_____

_____

Close and Check

Focus Question

How is dividing with mixed numbers related to dividing with whole numbers?
How is it related to dividing with fractions?

_____

_____

_____

_____

Do you know HOW?

1. Find $2\frac{2}{5} \div 1\frac{3}{5}$. Simplify the solution.

2. Each DVD is in a case. There are 12 cases in a box that is shipped to a video store. The contents of the box weigh $51\frac{3}{5}$ ounces. The weight of each DVD in its case is the same. How much does each DVD in its case weigh?

3. A carpenter is building sets of two picture frames. The first frame uses $7\frac{3}{5}$ inches of wood trim. The second frame uses $9\frac{1}{3}$ inches of trim. How many sets of picture frames can be made from 72 inches of trim? Simplify the quotient.

 sets

Do you UNDERSTAND?

4. Reasoning How can you use what you know about dividing fractions and mixed numbers to estimate a quotient?

_____

_____

_____

_____

_____

5. Error Analysis Explain the error and find the correct answer to the problem below.

$4\frac{3}{10} \div 2\frac{1}{5}$

$4 \div 2 = 2$ and $\frac{3}{10} \div \frac{1}{3} = \frac{3}{2}$

$2 + \frac{3}{2} = 3\frac{1}{2}$

_____

_____

_____

_____

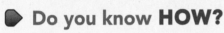

Problem Solving

Common Core Standards: 6.NS.1: Interpret and compute quotients of fractions, and solve word problems involving division of fractions by fractions, e.g., by using visual fraction models and equations to represent the problem.

Launch

A city plans a $\frac{1}{8}$-square-mile rectangular dog park. City workers bring $1\frac{1}{2}$ miles of fencing to build a fence around the park. After putting up one side of the fence, one worker says to the next, "I think we will need more fencing."

Do you agree? Explain.

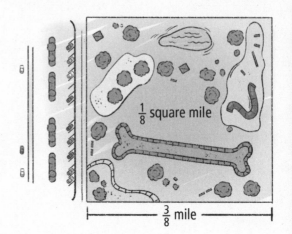

$\frac{1}{8}$ square mile

$\frac{3}{8}$ mile

Reflect

Would you rather divide by a fraction or multiply by a fraction? Can you always do what you want? Explain.

_____

_____

_____

_____

Close and Check

Focus Question

What kinds of real-world problems can be solved by dividing fractions?

_____

_____

_____

_____

▶ Do you know **HOW?**

1. A box of canned goods weighs 18 pounds. If each can weighs $14\frac{2}{5}$ ounces, how many cans are in the box?

 cans

2. What is the solution of $\frac{7}{9}d = \frac{2}{3}$?

3. The student council is creating a banner for a football game. The students will decorate $\frac{3}{8}$ of the banner, using $8\frac{1}{7}$ square feet. The remaining space will display the school name and mascot. How many total square feet is the banner?

4. The teachers make a $4\frac{5}{6}$ square foot banner, using $\frac{5}{6}$ of the total banner area. How many total square feet is the banner?

_____

▶ Do you **UNDERSTAND?**

5. Writing A riverboat travels 37 miles upstream, which is $\frac{4}{7}$ of the total trip. Show two different methods to find the total distance of the trip in miles.

_____

_____

_____

_____

6. Error Analysis Your uncle's motorcycle holds $9\frac{2}{5}$ gallons of gas and gets $53\frac{1}{3}$ miles per gallon. He says he can go $477\frac{2}{15}$ miles on a full tank. Explain his error and find how many miles he can travel on a tank of gas.

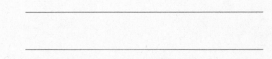

$9\frac{2}{5} \cdot 53\frac{1}{3} = 9 \cdot 53 + \frac{2}{5} \cdot \frac{1}{3} =$

$477 + \frac{2}{15} = 477\frac{2}{15}$

_____

_____

_____

_____

Adding and Subtracting Decimals

Common Core State Standards: 6.NS.3: Fluently add, subtract, multiply, and divide multi-digit decimals using the standard algorithm for each operation.

Launch

Your friend hands $20 to a circus store clerk and says, "I know exactly how much change you owe me for these, clown." The clerk replies, "Don't you want the deluxe noses, too? They blink."

Will the deluxe, decimal-priced, blinking noses change how your friend figures out her change? If so, how? And what will the change be?

All Prices Include Tax!

Reflect

Why do you use decimals with money?

_____

_____

_____

_____

Close and Check

Focus Question

How can you add and subtract decimals as easily as you do whole numbers?

_____

_____

_____

_____

Do you know HOW?

1. Find 26.054 + 5.7 + 0.92.

2. A shuttle bus travels 3.045 miles to the first bus stop. Then, the bus travels another 0.34 mile to the next stop. Finally, the bus travels 2.9 miles to the last stop. Find the total distance the bus travels.

3. Find 73.7 − 8.61.

4. Paper comes in a variety of thicknesses. A single sheet of card stock is 0.014 mm thick. Newsprint is only 0.0025 mm thick. What is the difference between the thickness of one sheet of cardstock and one sheet of newsprint?

Do you UNDERSTAND?

5. Writing What is the first step when adding and subtracting decimals? Explain why it is important.

_____

_____

_____

_____

6. Error Analysis Your friend says she ignores the decimal point when adding and subtracting decimals. After she finds the solution, she goes back and puts a decimal in the solution. Does this strategy work? Explain.

_____

_____

_____

_____

_____

Multiplying Decimals

Common Core State Standards: 6.NS.3: Fluently add, subtract, multiply, and divide multi-digit decimals using the standard algorithm for each operation.

Launch

Five bags of lemons and five boxes of cups arrive for your lemonade stand. Calculate the bill for each item. Explain the method you chose for calculating each bill.

Lemons	Lemonade cups

Reflect

Did you change your method of calculating each bill because one bill included a decimal-priced item and the other did not? Explain.

_____

_____

_____

Close and Check

Focus Question

How can you multiply decimals as easily as you multiply whole numbers?

_____

_____

_____

_____

Do you know HOW?

1. Find 0.041×0.07.

[ ]

2. A glass shop cuts a piece of replacement glass for a door. Find the area of the piece of glass.

27.5 in.

18.25 in.

[ ]

3. The price of gas is figured to the thousandth of a penny. The current price is $3.049 per gallon. A customer puts 7.45 gallons in her car. How much does she pay for the gas?

[ ]

Do you UNDERSTAND?

4. Reasoning Does the customer in Exercise 3 pay the exact price of the gas? Explain.

_____

_____

_____

_____

5. Error Analysis Your friend says that when multiplying decimals, you must place zeros at the end of the number so both factors have the same number of decimal places. Do you agree? Explain.

_____

_____

_____

_____

Dividing Multi-Digit Numbers

Common Core State Standards: 6.NS.2: Fluently divide multi-digit decimals using the standard algorithm.

Launch

Well, life gave your two friends lemons, 56 lemons in fact. They need 4 lemons for every pitcher of lemonade.

Find the number of pitchers of lemonade they can make. You can use any method but the standard long division method.

Reflect

Are there any benefits to doing a division problem using a method other than the standard long division method? Explain.

_____

_____

_____

_____

Close and Check

Focus Question

How can you use place value to divide any two whole numbers?

_____

_____

_____

_____

Do you know HOW?

1. Find 8,593 ÷ 12.

2. Find 4,697 ÷ 23.

3. A large apartment complex contains 55,000 square feet of living space. There are 132 individual apartments. What is the average number of square feet per apartment?

4. Windsor Castle is the largest inhabited castle in the world. It has 484,000 square feet of living space. There are 150 people in permanent residence in the castle. What is the average number of square feet per permanent resident?

Do you UNDERSTAND?

5. Reasoning Explain why it is important to be able to apply the arithmetic method of long division rather than drawing models to find quotients.

_____

_____

_____

_____

6. Error Analysis Identify the error in the division problem. What is the correct quotient?

$$
\begin{array}{r}
1150 \text{ R}17 \\
26\overline{)3007} \\
-26 \\
\hline
40 \\
-26 \\
\hline
147 \\
-130 \\
\hline
17
\end{array}
$$

_____

_____

_____

Dividing Decimals

Common Core State Standards: 6.NS.3: Fluently add, subtract, multiply, and divide multi-digit decimals using the standard algorithm for each operation.

Launch

Divide 50.4 by 3 without using the standard long division method.

Show your method. Tell what you like and don't like about your method.

Reflect

Do you like your method or the long division method better for dividing? Explain.

_____

_____

_____

_____

Close and Check

Focus Question

How can you divide decimals as easily as you divide whole numbers?

_____

_____

_____

_____

Do you know HOW?

1. Find 24.15 ÷ 6.

☐

2. Find 8.183 ÷ 83.5.

☐

3. There is 197.625 square feet of floor space in the back of a moving van. The van is 7.75 feet wide. Find the length of the space in the back of the van.

☐

4. A grocer orders boxes of macaroni and cheese for the store. The shelf is 8.43 feet wide. Each box is 0.125 foot wide. Find the number of boxes that will fit in each row on the shelf.

☐

Do you UNDERSTAND?

5. Reasoning Is it always possible to find an exact quotient when dividing with decimals? Explain.

_____

_____

_____

_____

6. Error Analysis A classmate says you can change decimal division to whole number division by moving the decimals to the end of both numbers before dividing. Do you agree with this problem-solving strategy? Explain.

_____

_____

_____

_____

_____

Common Core State Standards: 6.NS.7: Understand ordering and absolute value of rational numbers.

Launch

Use at least one decimal and at least one fraction to represent the quantity shown in four new and different ways. Tell whether one of these representations is more useful than the others and why.

> **four hundredths**

Reflect

Which offers you more possibilities to represent the same quantity in different ways – fractions or decimals? Explain.

_____

_____

_____

_____

Close and Check

> ## Focus Question
> When might you want to communicate a fraction as a decimal? When might you want to communicate a decimal as a fraction?
>
> _____
>
> _____
>
> _____
>
> _____

◗ Do you know **HOW?**

1. The area of land in the United States is about 0.052 of the total area of land on Earth. What fraction of total land on Earth does the United States make up?

2. A math class surveys the students in the school. The survey shows the $\frac{5}{8}$ of the students ride the bus to school on a regular basis. Write the fraction as a decimal.

3. The U.S. currency exchange rate determines the value of foreign dollars. If 1 U.S. dollar equals 12 foreign dollars, the value of the foreign currency is $\frac{1}{12}$ the value of U.S. currency. Write the fraction as a decimal to the nearest hundredth.

◗ Do you **UNDERSTAND?**

4. Writing Think of one real-world example when fractions are primarily used and one example when decimals are primarily used. Explain why each form is used in that situation.

_____

_____

_____

_____

_____

_____

5. Reasoning One student uses multiplication to find the decimal equivalent of $\frac{17}{20}$. Another student uses division. Which student is correct? Explain.

_____

_____

_____

_____

Comparing and Ordering Decimals and Fractions

Common Core State Standards: 6.NS.7: Understand ordering and absolute value of rational numbers.

Launch

 Complete the number line by adding and labeling at least two more tick marks at regular intervals. Then, place and label points on the number line at the following locations: 2.1, $2\frac{1}{3}$, 2.75, $2\frac{5}{8}$.

Explain the decisions you made.

2

Reflect

What did you consider most important about how you made your number line?

_____

_____

_____

_____

Close and Check

Focus Question

Which are usually easier to compare and order, fractions or decimals? Why?

_____

_____

_____

_____

▶ Do you know **HOW?**

1. Write the numbers in order from least to greatest.

Least

75.93 [   ]

75.9 [   ]

75.902 [   ]

75.951 [   ]

Greatest

2. Compare the fraction and decimal by using >, <, or = to make the statement true.

0.29 [   ] $\frac{2}{9}$

3. Circle the number in the box that could replace the question mark so that the numbers are ordered from least to greatest.

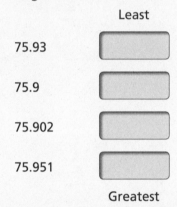

$\frac{3}{4}$ 0.32 $\frac{2}{3}$ 0.43

0.14, $\frac{1}{4}$, ?, $\frac{2}{5}$

▶ Do you **UNDERSTAND?**

4. Writing Describe a real-world situation in which you compare fractions and a situation in which you compare decimals.

_____

_____

_____

_____

_____

_____

5. Error Analysis You have finished $\frac{8}{9}$ of your science project. Your friend has finished 0.9 of her project. You say your project is more complete than your friend's project. She disagrees. Who is correct? Explain.

_____

_____

_____

_____

Problem Solving

Common Core State Standards: 6.NS.7: Understand ordering and absolute value of rational numbers. **6.EE.7:** Solve real-world and mathematical problems by writing and solving equations of the form $x + p = q$ and $px = q$ for cases in which p, q and x are all nonnegative rational numbers.

Launch

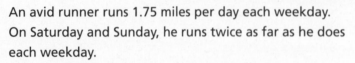

An avid runner runs 1.75 miles per day each weekday. On Saturday and Sunday, he runs twice as far as he does each weekday.

How many miles does he run each week? Show how you know.

Reflect

Would the problem have been easier, harder, or about the same if the runner ran whole number distances? Explain.

_____

_____

_____

_____

Close and Check

Focus Question

What kinds of problems can you solve using equations with decimals?

_____

_____

_____

_____

Do you know HOW?

1. A store sells team sweatshirts for $32.95. This is $7.36 more than the competitor's price on the same sweatshirt. Find the cost of the competitor's sweatshirt.

[ ]

2. Five friends earn a total of $127.20 doing odd jobs on the weekend. Each friend gets an equal share s of the earnings. Write a multiplication equation to represent the situation.

[ ]

3. Circle the expressions that are equivalent to $62.4\overline{)12.48}$.

$124.8 \div 624$ $\qquad$ $\dfrac{2}{100}$

$624\overline{)1248}$ $\qquad$ $\dfrac{1}{5}$

4. A quilt pattern calls for $\frac{7}{8}$ yard of blue fabric and 0.75 yard of yellow fabric. How many total yards of blue and yellow fabric are needed to make 3 quilts?

[ ] yards

Do you UNDERSTAND?

5. Compare and Contrast The friends in Exercise 2 decide to invest $\frac{1}{6}$ of the earnings in their small business. Explain how to set up the equation to show how much money is left to be shared equally among the 5 friends.

_____

_____

_____

_____

_____

6. Reasoning A woman walks 0.6 of a 2-mile track. Another woman walks $\frac{4}{5}$ of the same track. Which woman walks farther? Explain.

_____

_____

_____

_____

_____

_____

Integers and the Number Line

Common Core State Standards: 6.NS.5: … use positive and negative numbers to represent quantities in real-world contexts … . **6.NS.6.a:** Recognize opposite signs of numbers as indicating locations on opposite sides of 0 on the number line … . Also, **6.NS.6** and **6.NS.6.c.**

Launch

To prepare for an overnight camping trip, you begin checking the temperature to see what clothes to bring.

If the trend continues, what might the temperature be at 8 P.M.?

Describe or show a possible temperature.

Time	Temperature
4 P.M.	6°F
5 P.M.	5°F
6 P.M.	2°F
7 P.M.	0°F
8 P.M.	??

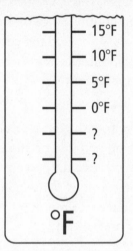

Reflect

Why do you need numbers less than zero?

_____

_____

_____

_____

Close and Check

Focus Question

What are integers? Why do we need integers? What do integers allow you to do that whole numbers do not?

_____

_____

_____

_____

Do you know HOW?

1. Complete the number line.

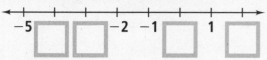

2. What is the opposite of −17?

3. What integer represents 6 strokes below par in golf?

4. A man enters a parking garage at street level (0). He parks on a level that is 4 floors below the street. What integer can represent where the man parked?

Do you UNDERSTAND?

5. Vocabulary How do you know that 8 and −8 are opposites?

_____

_____

6. Reasoning What integer can represent the position of the bait below the water line? Explain.

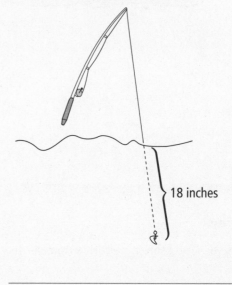

18 inches

_____

_____

_____

_____

Comparing and Ordering Integers

Common Core State Standards: 6.NS.7.a: Interpret statements of inequality as statements about the relative position of two numbers on a number line diagram . . . . **6.NS.7.b:** Write, interpret, and explain statements of order for rational numbers in real-world contexts . . . . Also, **6.NS.7.**

Launch

The world's top four video game players square off in a new game called Zombie Pretzel Attack 2! Rank the final scores of the players. Explain how you decided.

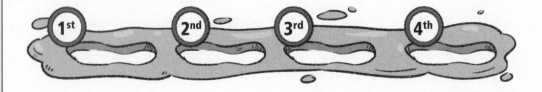

Reflect

How do you score a negative number like −100 in a game?

_____

_____

_____

_____

Close and Check

Focus Question

What does it mean for one negative number to be greater than another negative number? How can you use that information?

_____

_____

_____

_____

Do you know HOW?

In Exercises 1 and 2, write the symbol < or > that correctly completes each statement.

1. −12 [ ] −10

2. −12 [ ] −15

3. Each day, the stock market records the changes in stock values for investors.

Stocks	Net Change
Computer	10
Health Care	−3
Financial	5
Airlines	−20
Energy	−8

Order the integers from least to greatest.

    [ ]

Do you UNDERSTAND?

4. Reasoning Is −5 to the left or right of −8 on a number line? How does this help you know which integer is greater?

_____

_____

_____

_____

_____

5. Writing In golf, the player with the lowest score wins. Player A scores a −1. Player B scores a −5. Explain how you know that Player B wins.

_____

_____

_____

_____

_____

_____

Absolute Value

Common Core State Standards: 6.NS.7.b: Write … statements of order for rational numbers … .
6.NS.7.c: Understand the absolute value of a rational number as its distance from 0 on the number line … .
6.NS.7.d: Distinguish comparisons of absolute value from statements about order … . Also, **6.NS.7.**

Launch

Two discus throwers try out for the track team. Thrower 1 throws the discus forward, but Thrower 2 slips and throws the discus the wrong way.

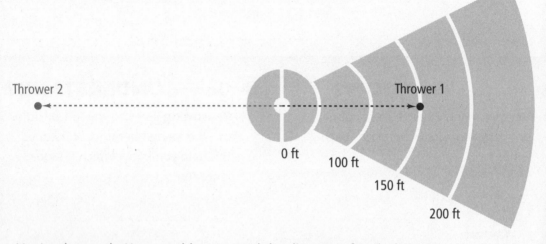

You're the coach. How would you record the distance of each throw? Who threw the discus farther? Who would you choose for the team?

Reflect

What is the shortest distance a discus can travel?

_____

_____

_____

Close and Check

Focus Question

How can you express the distance of any number from 0? When might you need to know the distance from 0?

_____

_____

_____

_____

Do you know **HOW?**

In Exercises 1 and 2, find each absolute value.

1. $|2|$

2. $|-13|$

3. Order the values from least to greatest.

$-9, 7, |-3|, 0, |1|$

4. Which number has a greater absolute value, -3 or -7?

5. The Dead Sea Depression near Israel has an elevation of 422 meters below sea level. Death Valley, CA has an elevation of 86 meters below sea level. Write an integer that represents the place with the lower elevation.

Do you **UNDERSTAND?**

6. Reasoning If two different integers have the same absolute value, what do you know about the integers? Explain.

_____

_____

_____

7. Error Analysis Suppose a number line represents your street. Each mile of your street is represented by an integer. Your house is located at 0. Your friend lives no more than 2 miles from you. He says his house is located at -3. Is your friend correct? Explain.

_____

_____

_____

_____

Integers and the Coordinate Plane

Common Core State Standards: 6.NS.6.b: Understand signs of numbers in ordered pairs as indicating locations in … the coordinate plane; recognize that when two ordered pairs differ only by signs, the locations of the points are related by reflections across one or both axes. Also, **6.NS.6, 6.NS.6.c, 6.NS.8.**

Launch

Write the missing coordinates (?, ?) for points *A*, *B*, and *C*. Explain how you know you are right.

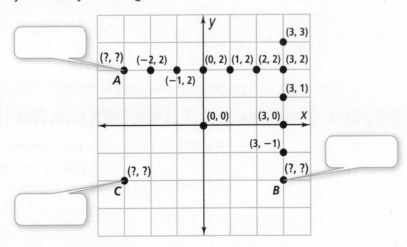

Reflect

How does the numbering of coordinates relate to your earlier work on integers on the number line?

_____

_____

_____

_____

Close and Check

> ## Focus Question
>
> How is a number line related to the coordinate plane? How are integers used within the coordinate plane?
>
> _____
>
> _____
>
> _____
>
> _____

▶ Do you know HOW?

Use the coordinate plane for Exercises 1-4.

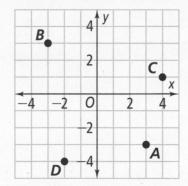

1. Plot points $X(2, 3)$, $Y(-4, 2)$, and $Z(-3, -1)$ on the coordinate plane.

2. What are the coordinates of point D?

3. In what quadrant does point D lie?

4. What is the reflection of $(3, -3)$ across the x-axis?

▶ Do you UNDERSTAND?

5. Compare and Contrast Explain how the coordinates of a point and its reflection across the x-axis are the same and how they are different.

_____

_____

_____

6. Error Analysis Your classmate identifies the coordinates of point $P(1, -3)$. Explain the error.

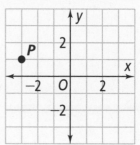

_____

_____

_____

_____

8-5 Distance

Common Core State Standards: 6.NS.8: ... Include use of coordinates and absolute value to find distances between points with the same first ... or ... second coordinate. **6.G.3:** ... use coordinates to find the length of a side joining points with the same first ... or ... second coordinate ... .

Launch

A park worker gets a call from her boss who says, "Build a rectangular sandbox with your 20 feet of board. Put a corner at (0, 0), (0, 5), (4, 0), and... ." The phone goes dead.

Show how the worker can plot the sandbox on the grid without calling her boss back. Tell why she has more than enough board.

Playground Grid Plan

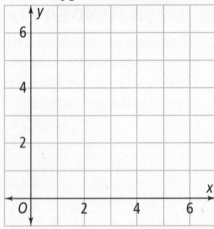

Reflect

Why would a grid be useful when planning to build a sandbox at a playground?

_____

_____

_____

_____

Close and Check

Focus Question

How are integers used to express distance? What does a negative number mean when you are talking about distance?

_____

_____

_____

_____

Do you know HOW?

1. What is the distance between the points (10, −8) and (10, 8)?

2. What is the distance between the points (10, 3) and (−2, 3)?

3. You draw a square diagram of your science project on a coordinate grid. The corners of the diagram are located at (5, −4), (−2, −4), (−2, 3), and (5, 3). How many units long is each side of the diagram?

4. The distance between two points is 10. The coordinates of one point are (3, −4). Fill in the y-coordinate of the second point, which is in Quadrant I.

(3, ☐)

Do you UNDERSTAND?

5. Writing Find the perimeter and area of the square diagram in Exercise 3. Explain how you found your answer.

_____

_____

_____

_____

6. Error Analysis There are two points on a coordinate grid at (7, 12) and (7, −5). A classmate says the distance between the two points is 7. Tell whether your classmate is correct. Explain your reasoning.

_____

_____

_____

_____

_____

Problem Solving

Common Core State Standards: 6.NS.6.b: ... recognize that when two ordered pairs differ only by signs, the locations of the points are related by reflections across ... axes. **6.NS.7.c:** ... interpret absolute value as magnitude for a positive or negative quantity in a real-world situation ... . Also, **6.G.3.**

Launch

Draw your own go-cart racecourse that starts and finishes at the clubhouse, forms a rectangle, passes by another given point on one turn, and is 24 blocks long. Each grid line represents 1 block.

Label the coordinates on each turn. Explain why your racecourse works.

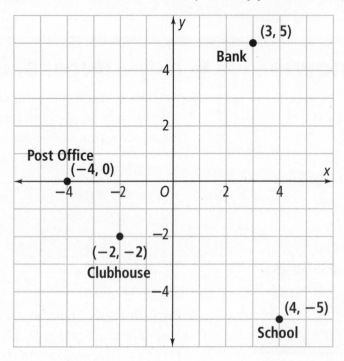

Reflect

Can the drivers ever go a negative distance? Explain.

_____

_____

Close and Check

Focus Question

In this topic you have learned different ways to use integers. How do integers help you to solve problems?

_____

_____

_____

_____

▶ Do you know **HOW?**

Use the story for Exercises 1-3.

The mail carrier walks 6 blocks on her route before noticing she has dropped a package. She walks back 4 blocks and finds it on the ground. She continues her route, walking 10 blocks. She decides she needs a bottle of water, so she goes back 2 blocks to a corner store. After finishing her water, she walks another 15 blocks to complete her route.

1. Describe the mail carrier's route in integers.

[ ] [ ] [ ] [ ] [ ]

2. How many blocks did the mail carrier walk?

[ ]

3. How many actual blocks is the mail carrier's route?

[ ]

▶ Do you **UNDERSTAND?**

4. Reasoning The map of your town is on a coordinate grid. Each square is a town block. The town center at is the origin. If your house is located at $(-10, 0)$, explain how -10 and $|-10|$ can both represent where you live.

_____

_____

_____

5. Writing Point $(-3, 5)$ is reflected across the x-axis, and then the image is reflected across the y-axis. The same point $(-3, 5)$ is reflected across the y-axis, and then the image is reflected across the x-axis. What do you know about the final images? Is this true for any point?

_____

_____

_____

Rational Numbers and the Number Line

Common Core State Standards: 6.NS.5: ... Use positive and negative numbers to represent quantities in real-world contexts ... . **6.NS.6.a:** Recognize opposite signs of numbers as indicating locations on opposite sides of 0 on the number line ... . Also, **6.NS.6** and **6.NS.6.c.**

Launch

The skateboard club's exacting executive manager creates a new scoring system for the boarders' moves. The boarders say the system is suspect because "none of our scores land on a number."

Do you agree with the boarders? What could their scores be? Explain.

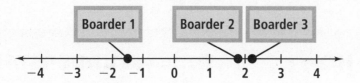

Reflect

How many scores do you think are between 0 and 1? Explain.

_____

_____

_____

_____

Close and Check

> ## Focus Question
>
> What are rational numbers? How can you use rational numbers?
>
> _____
>
> _____
>
> _____
>
> _____

▶ Do you know HOW?

1. What rational number is the opposite of point *R*?

2. Altitude is measured in relation to sea level, which is 0. Circle the rational number(s) that represents a position below sea level.

A. −2,480 ft

B. 503 ft

C. $1,403\frac{2}{3}$ ft

D. $-729\frac{1}{2}$ ft

3. In golf, scores are recorded in relation to par, which is 0. Write each score as a rational number.

Golfer	A	B	C
Score (par)	3 under	4 over	1 under
Rational Number			

▶ Do you UNDERSTAND?

4. Vocabulary Explain the difference between rational numbers and integers.

_____

_____

_____

_____

_____

_____

5. Error Analysis A friend says −3.7 is not a rational number because it isn't written in the form $-\frac{a}{b}$. Do you agree? Explain.

_____

_____

_____

_____

_____

Comparing Rational Numbers

Common Core State Standards: 6.NS.7.b: Write, interpret, and explain statements of order for rational numbers in real-world contexts . . . . **6.NS.7.c:** Understand the absolute value of a rational number as its distance from 0 on the number line . . . . Also, **6.NS.7** and **6.NS.7.a.**

Launch

On the second day of skateboard practice, Boarder 1 asks the exacting executive manager for a verbal description of her score and how it compares to the other boarders' scores. Boarder 1 doesn't want her exact score if it's not a whole number.

Describe Boarder 1's score and how it compares to the other boarders' scores without saying Boarder 1's score.

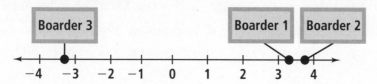

Description of Boarder 1's score:

How Boarder 1 compares to Boarder 2:

How Boarder 1 compares to Boarder 3:

Reflect

How could you let Boarder 1 know her exact score for sure without giving her the score? Explain.

_____

_____

_____

_____

Close and Check

Focus Question

What does it mean for one rational number to be greater than another rational number? How can you compare absolute values of rational numbers?

_____

_____

_____

_____

Do you know HOW?

Use the number line for Exercises 1 and 2.

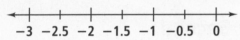

−3 −2.5 −2 −1.5 −1 −0.5 0

1. Write the symbol $<$, $>$, or $=$ to compare the pair of rational numbers.

$-2\frac{3}{4}$ ☐ -2.7

2. Write the symbol $<$, $>$, or $=$ to compare the absolute values of the pair of rational numbers.

$\left|-2\frac{3}{4}\right|$ ☐ $|-2.7|$

3. After reaching the summit, a climbing expedition descends the mountain in two groups. Circle the group that is farthest from the summit.

Group	A	B
Position relative to summit	−675 ft	−831 ft

Do you UNDERSTAND?

4. Reasoning You want to find which is greater, the total amount of savings account deposits or the total amount of withdrawals. Would you use the rational numbers or their absolute values? Explain.

_____

_____

_____

_____

5. Error Analysis A classmate says the value and the absolute value of a number are the same. Do you agree? Explain.

_____

_____

_____

_____

_____

Ordering Rational Numbers

Common Core State Standards: 6.NS.7: Understand ordering and absolute value of rational numbers.
6.NS.7.a: Interpret statements of inequality . . . . **6.NS.7.b:** Write, interpret, and explain statements of order for rational numbers in real-world contexts . . . .

Launch

The skateboard manager posts her final boarder ratings. After much complaint, she deducts a half point and then posts each boarder's completely final rating.

Draw a line from the Boarders' scores to order the Completely Final Ratings. Tell if you would have solved the problem differently if the ratings were integers instead of rational numbers.

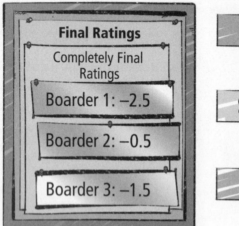

Final Ratings

Completely Final
Ratings

Boarder 1: −2.5

Boarder 2: −0.5

Boarder 3: −1.5

  First

 **Second**

 **Third**

Reflect

What's the most important thing about ordering any kind of numbers—whole numbers, integers, or rational numbers?

_____

_____

_____

_____

Close and Check

Focus Question

How can you interpret the ordering of rational numbers in real-world situations?

_____

_____

_____

_____

Do you know HOW?

1. Write the numbers in order from least to greatest.

$$\frac{14}{5}, -2.46, -\frac{10}{4}, 2.5$$

[ ] , [ ] , [ ] , [ ]

2. Order the archeological excavation sites from the least depth to the greatest depth.

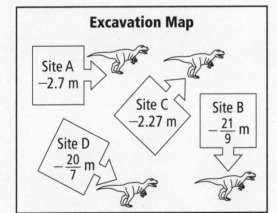

Excavation Map

Site A −2.7 m

Site C −2.27 m

Site B −$\frac{21}{9}$ m

Site D −$\frac{20}{7}$ m

Site [ ] Site [ ] Site [ ] Site [ ]

Do you UNDERSTAND?

3. Reasoning How might using absolute value be helpful when ordering negative rational numbers?

_____

_____

_____

_____

4. Error Analysis A classmate ordered these numbers from greatest to least. What error did she make? Explain.

$$4.4, 4.2, -4.42, -4.24$$

_____

_____

_____

_____

_____

Rational Numbers and the Coordinate Plane

Common Core State Standards: 6.NS.6.b: Understand signs of numbers in ordered pairs as indicating locations in quadrants of the coordinate plane; recognize that when two ordered pairs differ only by signs, the locations of the points are related by reflections across one or both axes. Also, **6.NS.6** and **6.NS.6.c.**

Launch

Write the missing coordinates (?, ?) for points *A* and *B*.

Explain how you know you are right.

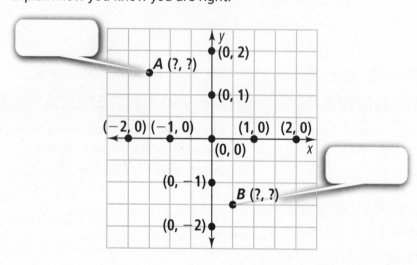

Reflect

How does the numbering of coordinates relate to your earlier work on rational numbers on the number line?

_____

_____

_____

Close and Check

Focus Question

How is a number line related to the coordinate plane? How are rational numbers used within the coordinate plane?

_____

_____

_____

_____

▶ Do you know **HOW?**

1. Write the coordinates for each point.

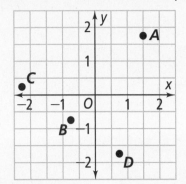

A: [ ]   B: [ ]

C: [ ]   D: [ ]

2. Plot and label the points on the coordinate grid.

$W(-2.25, -1.75)$ $X(1\frac{1}{4}, \frac{3}{4})$

$Y(-1.25, 2.25)$ $Z(1\frac{3}{4}, -2\frac{1}{4})$

3. Write the coordinates of point W reflected across the y-axis.

W: [ ]

4. Write the coordinates of point Z reflected across the x-axis.

Z: [ ]

▶ Do you **UNDERSTAND?**

5. Writing How would the signs of the coordinates of point X in Exercise 2 change if the point were reflected across the origin? Explain.

_____

_____

_____

_____

_____

6. Reasoning Point G is located at $(-1.23, 2.23)$. Compare the coordinates of point G and point Y. Is point G closer or farther away from the origin than point Y? Explain.

_____

_____

_____

_____

_____

Polygons in the Coordinate Plane

Common Core State Standards: 6.G.3: Draw polygons in the coordinate plane given coordinates for the vertices; use coordinates to find the length of a side joining points with the same first coordinate or the same second coordinate. Apply these techniques in the context of solving … problems.

Launch

A park worker has to use all 22 feet of board to make a square sandbox. She tries but all she can come up with is the plan as shown.

Tell what she got wrong and right. Then show a plan that does work. Include coordinates for your plan.

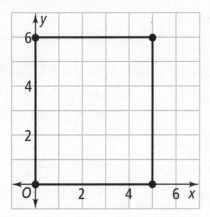

Reflect

Do you think objects in the real world use whole number measurements, rational number measurements, or both? Explain.

_____

_____

_____

_____

Close and Check

Focus Question

What makes a figure a polygon? Why might you want to draw a polygon in the coordinate plane?

_____

_____

_____

_____

▶ Do you know **HOW?**

1. Draw polygon *QRST* with vertices at $Q(-1\frac{3}{4}, 1\frac{1}{4})$, $R(1.25, 1.25)$, $S(1\frac{3}{4}, -2)$, $T(-1.75, -1.5)$.

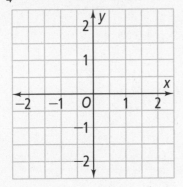

2. Find the length of segment *QR*.

3. Assume each unit of the grid represents 3.5 cm. Find the length of segment *QT*.

▶ Do you **UNDERSTAND?**

4. Reasoning Two students each draw a polygon using the same coordinates. One student says the perimeter of his figure is 12 units. The other student says the perimeter of her figure is 36 m. Can both students be correct? Explain.

_____

_____

_____

_____

5. Error Analysis A classmate writes an equation to find the distance between two points $X(-4.24, 3.39)$ and $Y(5.19, 3.39)$. Explain his error. Find the actual distance between the points.

$$-4.24 + 5.19 = 0.95$$

_____

_____

_____

Problem Solving

Common Core State Standards: 6.NS.7.b: Write, interpret, and explain statements of order for rational numbers in real-world contexts . . . . **6.G.3:** Draw polygons in the coordinate plane given coordinates for the vertices . . . . Also, **6.NS.6.b** and **6.NS.7.**

Launch

A famous artist starts planning four kite-shaped reflecting pools in a park. She wants each pool to be a reflection of the pool across from it on the *x* and *y* walking paths.

Draw and label the three other pools to finish the plan.

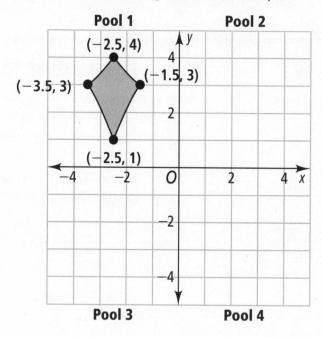

Reflect

What pattern do you see between the coordinates of the pools that are reflections of each other?

_____

_____

_____

_____

Close and Check

Focus Question

In this topic you have learned different ways to use rational numbers. How do rational numbers help you to solve problems?

Do you know HOW?

1. The diameter of a nail head must be less than 0.15 mm from the standard. Circle the nails that meet the requirement.

Difference from Standard	
Nail A	−0.14 mm
Nail B	+0.16 mm
Nail C	−0.15 mm
Nail D	+0.13 mm

2. A student started to draw trapezoid ABCD with vertices $A(-1\frac{1}{4}, 1\frac{3}{4})$ and $B(-2\frac{1}{4}, -2\frac{1}{4})$. Vertex C is a reflection of point B across the y-axis. Vertex D is a reflection of point A across the y-axis. What are the coordinates of point C and point D?

C:

D:

Do you UNDERSTAND?

3. **Reasoning** How much greater is the length of segment BC than segment AD in Exercise 2? Explain how you found you answer.

4. **Writing** Card games are often scored using integers. Is it possible to have more negative scores than your opponent and still win the game? Explain.

Ratios

Common Core State Standards: 6.RP.1: Understand the concept of a ratio and use ratio language to describe a ratio relationship between two quantities.

Launch

A gift shop sells boxes of fruit online, including this box of apples and pears. Use numbers to compare the fruit in three different ways.

Comparison 1	Comparison 2	Comparison 3

Reflect

Choose one of your comparisons. Describe a situation where you could use it.

_____

_____

_____

_____

Close and Check

Do you know HOW?

1. A sixth-grade band has 4 guitarists, 2 drummers, and 3 singers. Write a ratio for each comparison.

number of singers to
number of guitarists ☐ to ☐

number of guitarists
to number of
band members ☐ to ☐

number of drummers
to number of singers ☐ to ☐

2. For each ratio, tell what items are being compared.

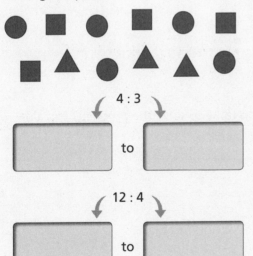

4 : 3

☐ to ☐

12 : 4

☐ to ☐

Do you UNDERSTAND?

3. Vocabulary What is a ratio?

4. Reasoning A class has 15 boys and 12 girls. Write at least three different ratios using this information.

5. Error Analysis Your friend says the ratio of the number of Hs to the number of Gs is 4 : 3. Is this correct? If not, tell what mistake he makes.

H   H   G   H
    G   G   G

Exploring Equivalent Ratios

Common Core State Standards: 6.RP.3: Use ratio and rate reasoning to solve real-world and mathematical problems, e.g., by reasoning about tables of equivalent ratios, tape diagrams, double number line diagrams, or equations.

Launch

A website sells song downloads for $2 each and movie downloads for $5 each. Your friend buys the same number of movies as songs. If he spends $20 on movies, how much does he spend on songs?

Use the multiplication table to show the solution.

x	1	2	3	4	5
1					
2					
3					
4					
5					

My friend buys ☐ songs and ☐ movies.

My friend spends ☐ on songs and ☐ on movies.

Reflect

Do you need to complete the whole multiplication table to solve the problem? Explain.

_____

_____

_____

_____

Close and Check

Focus Question

In this lesson, you learned about equivalent ratios. Can you use one ratio to write another ratio? Why might you want to do this?

_____

_____

_____

Do you know HOW?

1. Fill in three ratios equivalent to 2 : 3 on the multiplication table.

×	1	2	3	4
1				
2				
3				
4				

2. Make a domino with 12 dots and an equivalent ratio of dots on the left to dots on the right as the first domino. Use the multiplication table above to help.

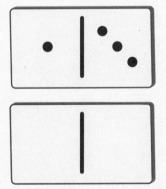

Do you UNDERSTAND?

3. **Reasoning** An animal shelter can hold only 60 cats and dogs. The current ratio of cats to dogs is 5 : 7. Can the shelter plan to take in more dogs and cats? Tell whether you know.

_____

_____

_____

_____

_____

4. **Writing** Describe a situation where you could use the ratio of cats to dogs to make a plan or decision at the shelter.

_____

_____

_____

_____

_____

Equivalent Ratios

Common Core State Standards: 6.RP.3: Use ratio and rate reasoning to solve real-world and mathematical problems, e.g., by reasoning about tables of equivalent ratios, tape diagrams, double number line diagrams, or equations.

Launch

The table shows votes for a new school team name. One friend says two grades voted the same. A second friend says the total vote for team name was the same.

Use ratios to show how both friends could be correct. Which team name should the school choose? Explain.

Votes for New Team Name

Grade	Wolves	Flyers
6th	20	10
7th	5	30
8th	30	15

· ·

The first friend is correct because:

· ·

The second friend is correct because:

· ·

The school should choose:

Reflect

How can ratios use different numbers but be the same?

_____

_____

_____

_____

Close and Check

Focus Question

What does it mean for two ratios to be equivalent? Why might you want to use an equivalent ratio?

Do you know HOW?

1. Complete the equivalent ratios on the double number line.

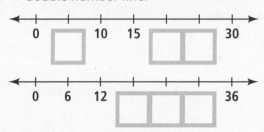

2. Each marble bag has a ratio of red to blue marbles of 3 to 4. You have 12 blue marbles. Complete the table to show how many marbles you have in your bag.

Number of Marbles

Red	Blue	Total
3	4	

I have [ ] marbles in my bag.

Do you UNDERSTAND?

3. Writing Tell how the ratios 6 : 2 and 3 : 1 describe a similar situation among the shapes.

4. Reasoning The ratio of consonants to vowels for two words are shown below. Explain how you can tell that the words are not the same.

Word One	Word Two
3 : 1	9 : 4

Ratios as Fractions

Common Core State Standards: 6.RP.1: Understand the concept of a ratio and use ratio language to describe a ratio relationship between two quantities. **6.RP.3:** Use ratio and rate reasoning to solve real-world and mathematical problems .... .

Launch

Due to high demand, a gift shop wants more fruit boxes with a 1 : 3 ratio of the number of apples to the total number of fruit.

Use letters to complete each plan. Write the fraction $\frac{\text{number of apples}}{\text{total number of fruit}}$. Cross out any plan that does not have the correct ratio.

b = banana   a = apple   p = pear   o = orange

Box Plan 2

Box Plan 1

Box Plan 3

☐ apples
☐ fruit

☐ apples
☐ fruit

☐ apples
☐ fruit

Reflect

How do the ratio and the fractions in the problem both describe the apples in the boxes?

_____

_____

_____

_____

Close and Check

Focus Question

Why might you want to write a ratio as a fraction?

_____

_____

_____

_____

Do you know HOW?

1. You propose a new mix of fruit for a fruit box. Write the ratio of apples to fruit (apples, pears, oranges, and mangoes) in three ways.

 to

 :

2. The ratio of rock songs to all songs on a playlist is $\frac{36}{60}$. Write this ratio in simplest form.

3. Circle the ratios that are equivalent to $\frac{36}{60}$.

$\frac{6}{10}$ $\frac{9}{15}$ $\frac{15}{20}$

$\frac{24}{36}$ $\frac{48}{80}$

Do you UNDERSTAND?

4. **Writing** Your class visits the zoo. Your friend says that the ratio of elephants to giraffes is $\frac{3}{8}$. You describe the relationship of elephants to giraffes as $\frac{9}{24}$. Can both you and your friend be correct? Explain.

_____

_____

_____

_____

5. **Compare and Contrast** How would the problem above have been the same or different if the ratios would have been written as 3 : 8 and 9 : 24? Explain.

_____

_____

_____

_____

_____

_____

_____

Common Core State Standards: 6.RP.1: Understand the concept of a ratio and use ratio language to describe a ratio relationship between two quantities. **6.RP.3:** Use ratio and rate reasoning to solve real-world and mathematical problems . . . .

Launch

Two students take turns recording daily rain totals. When the teacher sees their work, she exclaims, "Give me the daily results and total rainfall in one way!"

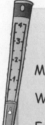

Student 1
Rain Totals

Monday: $\frac{1}{2}$ inch

Wednesday: $\frac{2}{10}$ inch

Friday: no rain

Student 2
Rain Totals

Tuesday: 0.3 inch

Thursday: 0.6 inch

Show how you would revise the results for the teacher.

Explain your work.

Reflect

Does it matter whether you choose decimals or fractions? Are there situations where using one is better than using the other?

_____

_____

_____

_____

Close and Check

Focus Question

Why might you want to write a ratio as a decimal?

_____

_____

_____

_____

Do you know HOW?

1. According to a recent study, the ratio of households in the United States that have high-speed Internet access is 0.64. Cross out the fractions that cannot be used to describe this ratio.

   $\frac{64}{100}$ $\frac{1}{64}$ $\frac{16}{25}$ $\frac{6}{4}$

2. Each row of the table shows a star basketball player's ratio of free throws made to free throws attempted. Complete the table. Circle the game with the best ratio.

Free Throw Ratios			
Game 1	7 : 8	$\frac{}{8}$	
Game 2	: 4	$\frac{3}{}$	0.75
Game 3	4 :	$\frac{4}{5}$	

3. In Game 4, the star player makes 0.6 of her free throws attempted. She attempts 5 free throws. How many did she make?

   [____] free throws

Do you UNDERSTAND?

4. **Writing** Describe why writing each ratio of free throws made as a decimal makes it easier to compare the ratios.

   _____

   _____

   _____

   _____

5. **Error Analysis** A study shows that approximately 0.08 of the population are left handed. Your friend says, "8 out of 10 people are left handed." What mistake does your friend make?

   _____

   _____

   _____

   _____

Problem Solving

Common Core State Standards 6.RP.1: Understand the concept of a ratio and use ratio language to describe a ratio relationship between two quantities. 6.RP.3: Use ratio and rate reasoning to solve real-world and mathematical problems . . . .

Launch

One hundred students vote for a drama, comedy, or action movie for a party. Drama gets one fifth of the votes. Action gets three times as many votes as comedy.

Write the vote totals.

All Votes: ☐   Drama: ☐   Action: ☐   Comedy: ☐

Tell which of these ratios correctly describe the results of the voting.

comedy votes to action votes   **1 to 3**

all votes to comedy votes   **5 ⊙ 1**

action votes to drama votes   **$\frac{3}{1}$**

action votes to all votes   **0.6**

Reflect Which ratio is the best for showing which movie type won the vote? Explain.

_____

_____

_____

Close and Check

Focus Question

In this topic you have learned different ways to work with ratios. How can you use what you learned to make plans and decisions?

_____

_____

_____

_____

Do you know HOW?

1. Your friend makes dough for a model volcano that turns out too dry. She changes the ratio of water to dry ingredients to 1 : 4. Then she doubles each ingredient to make more dough. Write the new ingredient amounts.

Volcano Dough Recipe

Item	Old Amounts	New Amounts
flour (cups)	3	
salt (cups)	1	
water (cups)	$\frac{1}{2}$	
cooking oil	2	

2. You can make green paint by mixing blue paint to yellow paint in a $\frac{3}{5}$ ratio. How many gallons of blue and yellow paint do you need to make 40 gallons of green paint?

Blue paint: ⬜ gallons

Yellow paint: ⬜ gallons

Do you UNDERSTAND?

3. Error Analysis For each class of 30 students, the ratio of boys to girls or girls to boys can be no more than 3 to 2. The principal plans Class A and B. What error does the principal make?

Class A	Class B
19 Boys	13 Boys
11 Girls	17 Girls

_____

_____

_____

4. Reasoning Tell how to fix the error by moving the fewest students between Class A and B. Each class must have 30 students.

_____

_____

_____

_____

Common Core State Standards: 6.RP.2: Understand the concept of a unit rate $\frac{a}{b}$ associated with a ratio $a : b$ with $b \neq 0$, and use rate language in the context of a ratio relationship ... . **6.RP.3:** Use ratio and rate reasoning to solve real-world and mathematical problems ... .

Launch

The label shows nutritional benefits for an entire 12-fluid-ounce sports drink. The beverage company wants to produce a 16-fluid-ounce bottle of the same drink.

How many calories and grams (g) of carbohydrates should the company put on the label?

Reflect How many calories does 1 fluid ounce of sports drink have? How would knowing this be useful?

_____

_____

_____

_____

Close and Check

Focus Question

What makes a ratio a rate? When could rates be useful?

_____

_____

_____

_____

Do you know HOW?

1. Write each as a rate and as a unit rate.

32 flowers to 8 vases

rate

unit rate

22 gallons to 5 buckets

rate

unit rate

4 boats to 20 days

rate

unit rate

2. The boat company makes 4 boats in 20 days. At that rate, how many boats could they make in 25 days?

boats

Do you UNDERSTAND?

3. Vocabulary How is a unit rate different from other rates?

_____

_____

_____

_____

_____

4. Error Analysis Your aunt works at a pet store that is about to receive a shipment of birds. She counts how many cages are available to know how many birds to place in each. She tells her boss the unit rate is 1 cage per 4 birds. Explain her mistake.

_____

_____

_____

_____

Unit Prices

Common Core State Standards: 6.RP.3.b: Solve unit rate problems including those involving unit pricing and constant speed. *For example, if it took 7 hours to mow 4 lawns, then at that rate, how many lawns could be mowed in 35 hours? At what rate were lawns being mowed?*

Launch

Your cousin shops for movies online. He sees three different offers.

Which offer should your cousin choose? Explain your reasoning.

Offer 1

Offer 2

Offer 3

Reflect Should you always choose the lowest unit rate? Why might your cousin *not* choose the lowest unit rate?

_____

_____

_____

_____

Close and Check

Focus Question

How can you compare the prices of different amounts of the same item? Why might you want to do this?

_____

_____

_____

_____

Do you know HOW?

1. If 5 gallons of gas costs $17.50, what is the unit price of the gas?

[   ]

2. A grocery store advertises weekly specials for fruit. Write the unit price for each type of fruit.

Weekly Specials

Fruit	Total Price	Unit Price
7 oranges	$3.01	
5 kiwis	$1.85	
9 plums	$2.88	
3 pears	$1.68	

3. A movie theater offers different ticket packages. Order them by the unit price for a ticket from greatest (1) to least (3).

Do you UNDERSTAND?

4. Reasoning 10 binders cost $1. 10 notebooks cost $1. Can you tell which is the better buy? Explain.

_____

_____

_____

5. Error Analysis Your friend says that the unit price of Pack A is lower because Pack A costs less than Pack B. Explain your friend's error.

```
Pack A            Pack B
10 pencils        50 pencils
for $1            for $4
```

_____

_____

_____

_____

Constant Speed

Common Core State Standards: 6.RP.3.b: Solve unit rate problems including those involving unit pricing and constant speed. *For example, if it took 7 hours to mow 4 lawns, then at that rate, how many lawns could be mowed in 35 hours? At what rate were lawns being mowed?*

Launch

Three riders try out for one spot on a bike team with different coaches for different distances with different times.

What factors should the coaches consider when picking a rider?
Which rider should they pick? Justify your choice.

Rider	Distance (miles)	Time (minutes)
Rider 1	5	20
Rider 2	6	30
Rider 3	8	40

Factors to Consider:

The Rider to Pick:

Reflect What could the coaches have done to make the try-outs better?

Close and Check

Focus Question

What is the relationship between distance and time? How can you use this relationship?

_____

_____

_____

_____

Do you know HOW?

1. Millions of monarch butterflies migrate from Canada to Mexico each year. They travel at an average rate of 12 miles per hour. How far will the butterflies travel in 7 hours?

2. Some monarch butterflies complete the 1,800-mile journey in about 60 hours of flight time. What is their average speed?

3. If a bicyclist travels 3 miles in 15 minutes, how far will he travel in 25 minutes maintaining a constant speed?

4. You have completed 4 miles of a 10-mile race in 32 minutes. At this pace, how long will it take you to complete the entire race?

Do you UNDERSTAND?

5. **Writing** Two hikers start from the opposite ends of the same 18-mile trail. You know Hiker A's average speed r and Hiker B's finishing time t. Explain how you can determine which hiker completes the trail first.

_____

_____

_____

_____

6. **Reasoning** Your friend runs a 500-yard race with a goal to complete it in less than 3 minutes. If her average speed is 200 yards per minute, will she achieve her goal? Explain.

_____

_____

_____

Common Core State Standards: 6.RP.3.d: Use ratio reasoning to convert measurement units; manipulate and transform units appropriately when multiplying or dividing quantities.

Launch

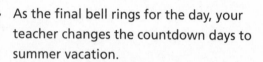

As the final bell rings for the day, your teacher changes the countdown days to summer vacation.

At the same time, your friend writes three ways other than days to count down the time in his notebook.

Show what he might have written.

Way 1	Way 2	Way 3

Reflect Which way would you use to keep track of time left until summer vacation? Explain.

_____

_____

_____

Close and Check

Focus Question

You can express measurements of time, length, weight, and capacity in many different units. Why would you want to convert measurements? How can rates help you find a common measurement?

_____

_____

_____

_____

Do you know HOW?

1. The average dairy cow produces 1,500 gallons of milk per year. The milk-bottling factory puts milk into quart bottles. About how many quarts of milk can it bottle each year from the average dairy cow?

   [_____] quarts

2. There are 1,760 yards in one mile. There are 2.54 centimeters in one inch. How many centimeters are there in one mile?

   [_____] centimeters

3. About how many meters tall is the tree? One inch is approximately 0.025 meter.

   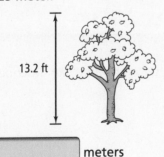

   13.2 ft

   [_____] meters

Do you UNDERSTAND?

4. **Error Analysis** Your aunt runs 3 miles in 30 minutes. Your uncle runs 4 kilometers in 30 minutes. He claims he ran farther. Explain why he is incorrect.

   _____

   _____

   _____

   _____

   _____

5. **Writing** Your best friend needs 150 centimeters of ribbon for his school project. At the store, he sees that ribbon is sold in spools of 60 inches. Explain how he can decide whether one spool is enough.

   _____

   _____

   _____

   _____

Choosing the Appropriate Rate

Common Core State Standards: 6.RP.3: Use ratio and rate reasoning to solve real-world and mathematical problems ... . **6.RP.3.b:** Solve unit rate problems including those involving unit pricing and constant speed ... .

Launch

Your mom and sister train for an upcoming family-fun foot race. Your mom says they're running 6 miles per hour. Your sister agrees saying they're running 10 minutes per mile.

Can they both be correct? Explain.

Reflect Are miles per hour and minutes per mile the only two rates that can describe how fast your mom and sister are running? Explain.

Close and Check

Focus Question

If you know two measurements, you can write two different rates. How do you know which rate is best to use in a situation?

_____

_____

_____

_____

Do you know HOW?

1. The presidential jet, Air Force One, can fly 10.5 miles per minute. How many miles per hour can Air Force One travel?

   [　　　　] miles per hour

2. How many hours would it take Air Force One to travel 2,268.6 miles from Washington, DC to San Diego, California?

   [　　　　] hours

3. A local plant nursery offers the following weekend deals. Circle the deal that offers the lowest price per plant.

Weekend Deals	
Deal 1	6 plants for $10
Deal 2	$7 for 4 plants
Deal 3	Buy 2 plants for $4, get one free
Deal 4	$1.50 per plant

Do you UNDERSTAND?

4. **Compare and Contrast** Your friend jumps rope at a rate of 25 jumps every minute. You know she jumped 85 times. If you want to know how many minutes she jumped rope, would you use the rate 25 jumps per minute or 1 minute per 25 jumps? Explain.

   _____

   _____

   _____

   _____

5. **Reasoning** You and a friend have to walk 0.85 mile to a play that begins in 20 minutes. You walk at a rate of 3.5 miles per hour. Is this the most useful way to write the rate to see if you will make it on time? Explain.

   _____

   _____

   _____

   _____

   _____

Problem Solving

Common Core State Standards: 6.RP.3: Use ratio and rate reasoning to solve real-world and mathematical problems, e.g., by reasoning about tables of equivalent ratios, tape diagrams, double number line diagrams, or equations.

Launch

A restaurant chain develops three possible slogans based on the number of people it serves. The chain has 10,000 restaurants and serves about 24 million people every day.

Is each slogan accurate using a 30-day month?

720 million people served every month

1 million people served every hour

100 people served per hour in each restaurant

Which slogan would you choose if you ran the company?

Reflect Why did you choose the slogan you chose?

_____

_____

Close and Check

Focus Question

In this topic, you have learned different ways to use rates. How do you use rates to make predictions and decisions?

_____

_____

_____

_____

Do you know HOW?

1. Your friend works 15 hours at the corner market and volunteers 780 minutes a week at the boys and girls club. Does your friend spend more time working or volunteering?

[ ]

2. The additional fees a cell phone company charges are shown below. How much extra can the customer expect to pay in a four-week period?

Additional Service	Fee per use	Additional Cost (per week)
3 additional minutes per day	$0.45	
2 ring tones each week	$1.99	
13 text messages each day	$0.05	
Total		

Four-week Total = [   ]

Do you UNDERSTAND?

3. Reasoning Describe a situation in which comparing unit rates is a useful problem-solving strategy and tell how you would apply the strategy.

_____

_____

_____

_____

4. Writing A member of the track team runs one mile in 7 minutes and 54 seconds. Use unit rates to find how fast he runs 4 miles at the same pace. Explain each step.

_____

_____

_____

_____

_____

Plotting Ratios and Rates

Common Core State Standards: 6.RP.3.a: Make tables of equivalent ratios relating quantities with whole number measurements ... and plot the pairs of values on the coordinate plane ... .
6.EE.9: ... Analyze the relationship between ... variables using graphs and tables ... .

Launch

An electronics company plans a 16-gigabyte model player that will hold the same ratio of songs to gigabytes of memory as their other players.

How many songs will the 16-gigabyte player hold? Tell how you know.

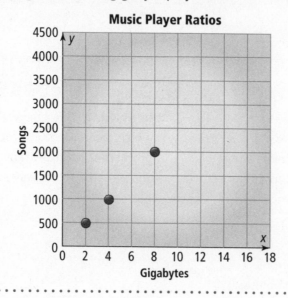

Music Player Ratios

Reflect

Did having the ratios plotted on a graph help you solve the problem? Explain.

_____

_____

_____

_____

Close and Check

Do you know HOW?

1. A recipe calls for 3 cups of sugar for every stick of butter used. Complete the table below.

Sticks of Butter	Cups of Sugar
1	
3	
	15
6	

2. Make a graph of the information from the table above. Plot and label each point.

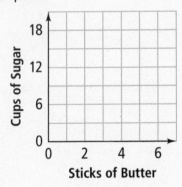

Do you UNDERSTAND?

3. **Reasoning** Could you use the graph in Exercise 2 to find how much sugar is needed for 4 sticks of butter? Explain.

_____

_____

_____

_____

4. **Compare and Contrast** Two friends analyze this equation. One friend says the volume of water increases $\frac{3}{4}$ ft^3 every minute. The other says the volume of water increases 3 ft^3 every 4 minutes. Which friend is correct? Explain.

$$y = \frac{3}{4}x$$
x = minutes
y = volume of water in cubic feet

_____

_____

_____

_____

Recognizing Proportionality

Common Core State Standards: 6.RP.2: ... Use rate language in the context of a ratio relationship ... .
6.RP.3: Use ratio and rate reasoning to solve real-world and mathematical problems ... .
6.RP.3.a: ... Plot the pairs of values on the coordinate plane ... .

Launch

You invent two robots to paint cars. Each robot works at a constant rate, but Robot 2 works faster than Robot 1.

Draw a line from the cards to the correct robot.

56 cars / 4 hours	48 cars / 4 hours
28 cars / 2 hours	
72 cars / 6 hours	36 cars / 3 hours
70 cars / 5 hours	

Tell how you know you're right.

Reflect

Could you predict how many cars Robot 2 would paint in only 1 hour? How?

_____

_____

_____

_____

Close and Check

> ## Focus Question
>
> A proportional relationship can be represented by equivalent ratios. How can you recognize proportional relationships in tables and graphs? Why is it important to be able to recognize proportional relationships in multiple ways?

Do you know HOW?

1. Circle the ratios that are proportional to $\frac{3}{4}$.

$\frac{6}{8}$ $\qquad$ $\frac{12}{16}$ $\qquad$ $\frac{13}{14}$

$\frac{36}{48}$ $\qquad$ $\frac{4}{3}$ $\qquad$ $\frac{15}{25}$

2. Circle each representation that shows a proportional relationship.

x	4	8	10	20	25
y	16	32	40	80	100

$\frac{8}{10}$ and $\frac{12}{16}$

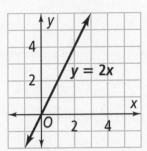

Do you UNDERSTAND?

3. Reasoning Explain why this graph does not represent a proportional relationship.

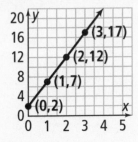

4. Error Analysis Explain the mistake in the following table of a proportional relationship.

x	12	32	45	80
y	3	8	11	20

Introducing Percents

Common Core State Standards: 6.RP.3.c: Find a percent of a quantity as a rate per 100 (e.g., 30% of a quantity means $\frac{30}{100}$ times the quantity); solve problems involving finding the whole, given a part and the percent.

Launch

Describe two part-to-whole situations that could relate to each ratio. Use words to describe one situation. Use a picture to describe the other situation.

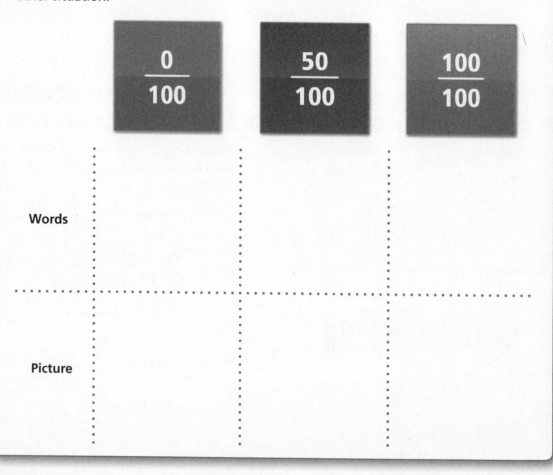

Words

Picture

Reflect

Would the task have been different if the ratios were $\frac{0}{92}$, $\frac{46}{92}$, and $\frac{92}{92}$? Explain.

_____

_____

_____

_____

Close and Check

Do you know HOW?

1. Look at the checkerboard below. What percent of the squares are white?

 %

2. Complete the table.

Ratio	Fraction	Percent
7 : 10	$\frac{}{100}$	70%
4 : 5	$\frac{}{100}$	%
8 :	$\frac{32}{100}$	%
: 50	$\frac{}{100}$	6%
9 :	$\frac{}{100}$	45%

Do you UNDERSTAND?

3. Writing How does using percents help when comparing the ratios 7 out of 20 and 11 out of 25?

_____

_____

_____

_____

_____

4. Error Analysis At a football game, 21 out of 25 people wore a red shirt. Your friend states that 4% of the people did not wear a red shirt. Explain the mistake your friend made. What percent of people did not wear a red shirt?

_____

_____

_____

_____

Using Percents

Common Core State Standards: 6.RP.3.c: Find a percent of a quantity as a rate per 100 (e.g., 30% of a quantity means $\frac{30}{100}$ times the quantity); solve problems involving finding the whole, given a part and the percent.

Launch

The teacher tells your friend she got 90% correct on a 20-question math quiz. Your friend says to you, "I think I got questions 5 and 17 wrong."

Is this possible? Tell how you know.

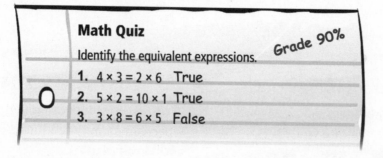

Math Quiz

Identify the equivalent expressions.   Grade 90%

1. $4 \times 3 = 2 \times 6$ True
2. $5 \times 2 = 10 \times 1$ True
3. $3 \times 8 = 6 \times 5$ False

Reflect

Would you rather have a teacher write your score on your paper as a percent or as a fraction? Does it matter? Explain.

_____

_____

_____

_____

Close and Check

Focus Question

Percents are another language you can use for comparisons. What does 100% represent? How are the terms of a ratio represented in a percent?

_____

_____

_____

Do you know **HOW?**

1. Complete each statement.

   [   ] is 95% of 20.

   [   ] is 60% of 10.

   [   ] is 30% of 50.

   [   ] is 40% of 25.

2. If 14 students choose red as their favorite color, how many students were surveyed?

Favorite Color

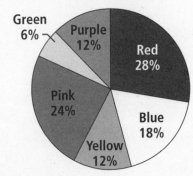

[   ] students

Do you **UNDERSTAND?**

3. **Reasoning** Can you determine the number of people who choose football as their favorite sport? Explain your reasoning.

Favorite Sport

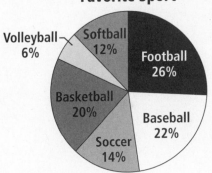

_____

_____

_____

4. **Error Analysis** Your friend said that 200 students were surveyed for the circle graph above and used it to conclude that 26 students chose football. What mistake did she make?

_____

_____

Problem Solving

Common Core State Standards: 6.RP.3: Use ratio and rate reasoning to solve real-world and mathematical problems, e.g., by reasoning about tables of equivalent ratios .... **6.RP.3.c:** Find a percent of a quantity as a rate per 100 .... .

Launch

The championship game is on the line. Which Wolves' basketball player should take the last shot? Explain.

Wolves Season Shooting Results

Player	Makes	Attempts
10	11	25
4	22	50
8	16	40
40	12	30
31	24	60

Reflect

Player #31 made the most shots. Should this player then take the last shot? Explain.

Close and Check

Focus Question

In this topic you have learned about percents and proportional relationships. How can you use percents and proportional relationships to solve problems?

_____

_____

_____

_____

Do you know HOW?

1. You have 30 coins in your bank. Complete the table.

Coin	Number	Percent
Quarter	6	
Dime		30%
Nickel		10%
Penny	12	

2. Using the table above, tell the ratio of nickels to dimes in simplest form.

3. At a local sporting event, the ratio of green shirts to yellow shirts was 3 : 5. If 160 people attended the sporting event, how many people were wearing green shirts?

_____ people

Do you UNDERSTAND?

4. Reasoning The ratio of cars to trucks in the parking lot is 5 to 3. Can you use just this information to determine the total number of vehicles in the parking lot?

_____

_____

_____

_____

5. Error Analysis The ratio of red marbles to green marbles in a bag is 3 : 4. Describe the mistake in the statement.

"If there are 120 red marbles, there must be 121 green marbles."

_____

_____

_____

_____

Rectangles and Squares

Common Core State Standards: 6.G.1: Find the area of right triangles, other triangles, special quadrilaterals, and polygons by composing into rectangles or decomposing into triangles and other shapes; apply these techniques in the context of solving real-world and mathematical problems.

Launch

Your friend uses small squares to make a rectangle and a square. Shape 1 uses 9 small squares, and Shape 2 uses 8 small squares.

Tell which shape is a rectangle and which is a square.

Shape 1 is a [   ]. Shape 2 is a [   ].

Then make and label each shape on the grid.

Reflect Can you make more than one possible rectangle? Can you make more than one possible square? Explain.

_____

_____

_____

_____

Close and Check

Focus Question
You find the area of a rectangle by multiplying its base and height. What happens to the area of a rectangle when you change its dimensions?

_____

_____

_____

_____

Do you know HOW?

1. What is the length of each side of the square?

A = 121 in.²

$s =$ _____

2. What is the width of the rectangle?

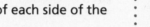

A = 31 ft²

$\ell = 7\frac{3}{4}$ ft

$w =$ _____

3. A square table has a side length of 1.52 m. What is the area of the table to the nearest hundredth meter?

_____

Do you UNDERSTAND?

4. Compare and Contrast Explain how finding the area of a square and the area of a rectangle are alike and different.

_____

_____

_____

_____

_____

5. Reasoning Three friends each drew a rectangle with an area of 18 in.². The rectangles each looked different no matter how the friends turned them. Explain how this is possible.

_____

_____

_____

_____

_____

Right Triangles

Common Core State Standards: 6.G.1: Find the area of right triangles, other triangles, special quadrilaterals, and polygons by composing into rectangles or decomposing into triangles and other shapes; apply these techniques in the context of solving real-world and mathematical problems.

Launch

The principal of a middle school wants students to help restore a nearby lot. The school asks each grade to submit a plan for part of the lot. The sixth grade plans a nature zone split evenly as shown between a garden and a mini-forest.

What is the area of each part of the nature zone? Explain.

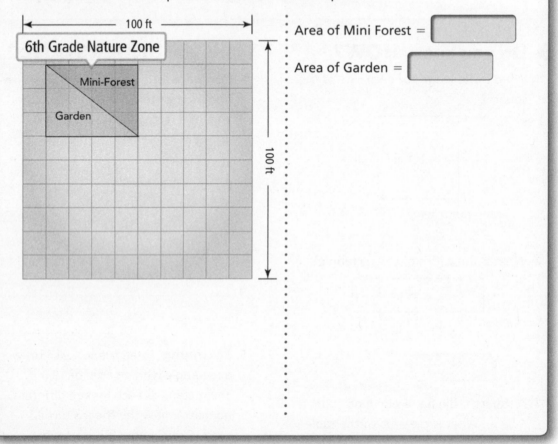

Area of Mini Forest =

Area of Garden =

Reflect How does knowing the area of a rectangle help you find the area of the two triangle-shaped spaces in the rectangle?

_____

_____

_____

_____

Close and Check

Do you know HOW?

1. Triangle Park takes up $\frac{1}{2}$ of a small, square city block. What is the area of Triangle Park?

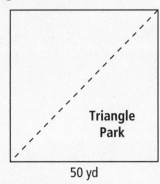

50 yd

2. A school banner is sewn in the shape of a right triangle. What is the area of the banner?

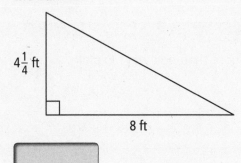

Do you UNDERSTAND?

3. Writing Describe two different ways you could solve Exercise 2.

4. Error Analysis A storeowner advertises a triangular deck kit. The owner lists the area of the deck. What error do you think the owner made?

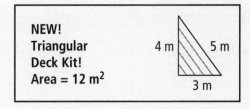

NEW! Triangular Deck Kit! Area = 12 m²   4 m   5 m   3 m

Parallelograms

Common Core State Standards: 6.G.1: Find the area of right triangles, other triangles, special quadrilaterals, and polygons by composing into rectangles or decomposing into triangles and other shapes; apply these techniques in the context of solving real-world and mathematical problems.

Launch

The seventh grade adds their plan for restoring the lot. They plan an art center shaped like a parallelogram for displaying student work.

What is the area of the art center? Explain.

100 ft

6th Grade Nature Zone

Mini-Forest

Garden

100 ft

7th Grade Art Center

Area of Art Center:

Reflect Can you find the area of the art center in more than one way? Explain.

_____

_____

_____

_____

_____

Close and Check

Focus Question

How can you show that the area formulas for parallelograms and rectangles are the same?

_____

_____

_____

_____

▶ Do you know **HOW?**

1. Draw lines to decompose the parallelogram into pieces that can be rearranged into a rectangle. Then find its area.

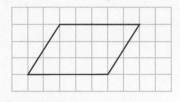

2. What is the area of the parallelogram?

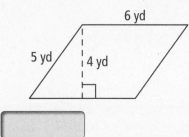

6 yd

5 yd   4 yd

3. A historical marker is in the shape of a parallelogram. The height is 5.7 m. The area of the marker is 22.8 m^2. What is the length of the base of the marker?

▶ Do you **UNDERSTAND?**

4. Reasoning Two teams make posters to show how to find the area of a parallelogram. Which team has the correct start? Explain.

Team A	Team B
We made two triangles and a rectangle to find the area!	We cut off the triangle on one side and taped it to the other to make a rectangle!

_____

_____

_____

_____

_____

Other Triangles

Common Core State Standards: 6.G.1: Find the area of right triangles, other triangles, special quadrilaterals, and polygons by composing into rectangles or decomposing into triangles and other shapes; apply these techniques in the context of solving real-world and mathematical problems.

Launch

The seventh grade changes their plan for the art center on the lot. They decide to split the art center into two triangle-shaped spaces as shown.

What is the area of the space devoted to paintings? Explain.

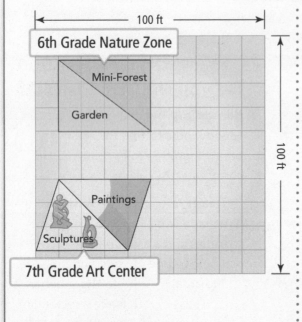

Area for paintings = [   ]

Reflect Suppose the seventh grade had split the art center by drawing a diagonal from the bottom left to the top right instead of what is shown. Would the area devoted to paintings be the same or different?

_____

_____

_____

_____

Close and Check

Focus Question

You can divide any parallelogram into two matching triangles. How is this useful?

► Do you know HOW?

1. What is the area of the acute triangle? Use the triangle to compose a parallelogram to find the area.

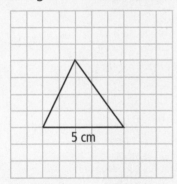

5 cm

2. Three houses share a yard in the shape of an obtuse triangle. What is the area of the triangular yard?

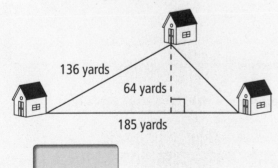

136 yards

64 yards

185 yards

► Do you UNDERSTAND?

3. Reasoning The perimeter of the parallelogram is 44 cm. Do you have enough information to find the area of one of the triangles? Explain.

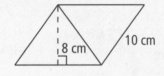

8 cm   10 cm

4. Vocabulary The height of a triangle can be inside a triangle, outside a triangle, or on the side of a triangle. Draw and label an example of each.

Common Core State Standards: 6.G.1: Find the area of right triangles, other triangles, special quadrilaterals, and polygons by composing into rectangles or decomposing into triangles and other shapes; apply these techniques in the context of solving real-world and mathematical problems.

Launch

The eighth grade adds their plan for restoring the lot. They plan a music center for student concerts in the shape of a pentagon.

What is the area of the planned music center? Explain.

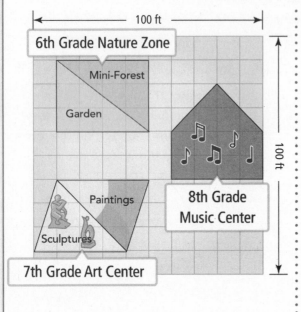

Area for Music Center = _____

Reflect Can you find the area of the music center in more than one way? Explain.

_____

_____

_____

_____

Close and Check

Focus Question

When you find the area of a polygon, how do you know whether to compose or decompose? Does it matter?

_____

_____

_____

_____

Do you know HOW?

1. What is the area of the trapezoid?

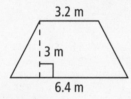

3.2 m

3 m

6.4 m

[ ]

2. A theater company uses a hexagonal stage that can be rotated to change scenes. What is the area of the entire stage?

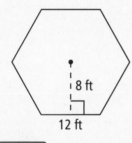

8 ft

12 ft

[ ]

Do you UNDERSTAND?

3. Reasoning Can you find the area of the stage in Exercise 2 by decomposing it into trapezoids? Explain.

_____

_____

_____

4. Writing Suppose that a part of the stage in Exercise 2 is removed to make room for the orchestra. Explain how you can find the area of the remaining stage.

_____

_____

_____

_____

_____

Problem Solving

Common Core State Standards: 6.G.1: Find the area of right triangles, other triangles, special quadrilaterals, and polygons by composing into rectangles or decomposing into triangles and other shapes; apply these techniques in the context of solving real-world and mathematical problems.

Launch

Combine some or all of the polygons to make a rectangle with an area of 20 square units.

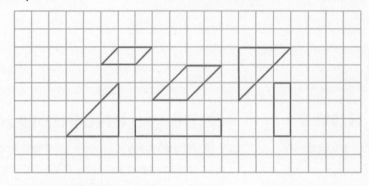

Draw your rectangle. Explain your work.

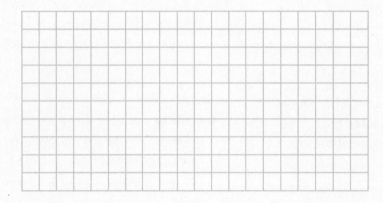

Reflect Describe a situation where you might rearrange polygons into a rectangle.

_____

_____

_____

_____

Close and Check

Focus Question

How can you find the area of any polygon? What does this allow you to do that you couldn't do before?

_____

_____

_____

_____

Do you know HOW?

1. What is the area of the polygon?

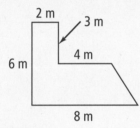

2. A picture is placed in to a wooden frame. The dimensions of the picture and frame are equivalent ratios. Find the area of the frame.

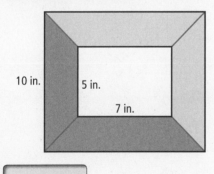

Do you UNDERSTAND?

3. Writing A homeowner wants to buy the exact amount of sod needed for her lawn. Describe what she needs to do.

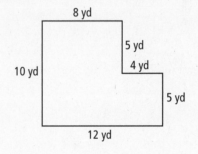

_____

_____

_____

4. Error Analysis Explain her mistake in calculating the amount of sod needed.

$A_1 = 10 \cdot 12 = 120 \text{ yd}^2$
$A_2 = 5 \cdot 4 = 20 \text{ yd}^2$
$A = 120 \text{ yd}^2 + 20 \text{ yd}^2 = \textbf{140 yd}^2$

_____

_____

_____

Analyzing Three-Dimensional Figures

Common Core State Standards: 6.G.4: Represent three-dimensional figures using nets made up of rectangles and triangles, and use the nets to find the surface area of these figures. Apply these techniques in the context of solving real-world and mathematical problems.

Launch

You play a "guess my word" card game with a friend. Your friend must name the figure on your card. You pick this card.

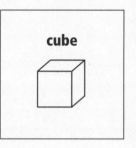

cube

Write at least five things you could say to get your friend to guess your word. You cannot use the word "cube" in your descriptions.

Reflect

Why is it useful to be able to describe solid figures?

_____

_____

_____

_____

Close and Check

Focus Question

What does it mean for a figure to be 3-D?

_____

_____

_____

_____

Do you know HOW?

1. Look at the following 3-D figures. Complete the table.

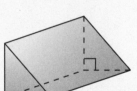

Figure 1   **Figure 2**

	Figure 1	Figure 2
Name		
Number of Faces		
Number of Edges		
Number of Vertices		
Shapes of Faces		

Do you UNDERSTAND?

2. Compare and Contrast How are a cube and a square pyramid alike? How are they different?

_____

_____

_____

_____

_____

3. Reasoning How many lateral faces does a pentagonal prism have? Explain.

_____

_____

_____

_____

Nets

Common Core State Standards: 6.G.4: Represent three-dimensional figures using nets made up of rectangles and triangles, and use the nets to find the surface area of these figures. Apply these techniques in the context of solving real-world and mathematical problems.

Launch

A toy store displays robotic dogs in cube-shaped boxes without fronts so kids can easily see what kind of dog is inside. A worker needs one more box. The boxes in the back room are all unfolded.

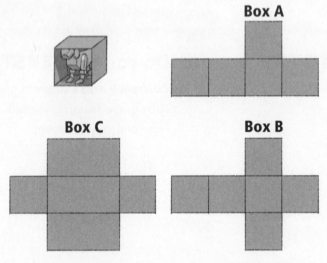

Box A

Box C

Box B

Can the worker choose a box without building it? Explain.

Reflect

How are the unfolded boxes useful?

_____

_____

_____

_____

Close and Check

Focus Question

How can you tell which 3-D figure a 2-D model will form?

_____

_____

_____

_____

Do you know HOW?

1. Name the three-dimensional figure the given net forms.

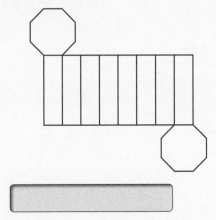

_____

2. Draw a net that forms a pentagonal pyramid.

Do you UNDERSTAND?

3. **Writing** Explain how you found your answer for Exercise 1.

_____

_____

_____

_____

_____

4. **Reasoning** A student wants to build a square pyramid using 2 squares and 3 triangles. Is this possible? Explain.

_____

_____

_____

_____

_____

Surface Areas of Prisms

Common Core State Standards: 6.G.4: Represent three-dimensional figures using nets made up of rectangles and triangles, and use the nets to find the surface area of these figures. Apply these techniques in the context of solving real-world and mathematical problems.

Launch

A box factory stamps out nets to make the cube-shaped robotic dog boxes. The manager shows the workers a sample net for the box.

The worker says, "Ok, I know how much cardboard I need for each box."

10 in.

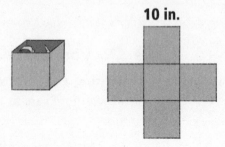

Explain how the worker knows.

Reflect

How does a net help you find how much cardboard was needed? Would the problem have been easier or harder if you just saw the folded box? Explain.

_____

_____

_____

Close and Check

Focus Question

How do you describe the surface area of a prism? How does the prism's net help you do that?

_____

_____

_____

_____

Do you know HOW?

1. Find the surface area of the figure below.

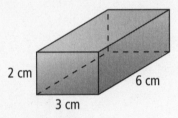

2. How many square inches of paper is needed to create the triangular prism shown below?

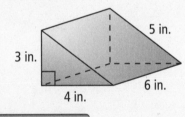

Do you UNDERSTAND?

3. Writing Explain how to find the surface area of a 3-D figure.

_____

_____

_____

_____

4. Error Analysis A student calculated the surface area of the figure below. What mistake did the student make? Find the correct surface area.

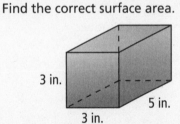

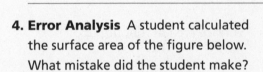

$6 \cdot (3)(3) = 6 \cdot 9 = 54$ in.^{2}

_____

_____

_____

_____

14-4 Surface Areas of Pyramids

Common Core State Standards: 6.G.4: Represent three-dimensional figures using nets made up of rectangles and triangles, and use the nets to find the surface area of these figures. Apply these techniques in the context of solving real-world and mathematical problems.

Launch

The toy company plans to sell their new robotic puppies in pyramid-shaped boxes instead of a cube-shaped box without a front.

A worker says, "I can tell which box will need more cardboard by just looking." Explain how the worker knows. Justify your response by finding the surface area of each box.

Robotic Dog Box   **Robotic Puppy Box**

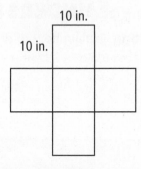 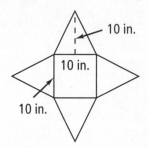

Surface area of robotic dog box:

Surface area of robotic puppy box:

How the worker knows:

Reflect

How does this problem relate to your past work on composing and decomposing shapes?

_____

_____

_____

Close and Check

Focus Question

How do you describe the surface of a pyramid? How does the pyramid's net help you do that?

_____

_____

_____

_____

Do you know HOW?

1. What is the surface area of the figure below?

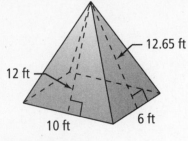

- 12.65 ft
- 12 ft
- 10 ft
- 6 ft

2. A triangular pyramid is made using 4 equilateral triangles. The net is shown below.

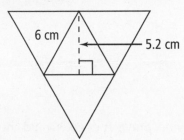

- 6 cm
- 5.2 cm

What is the surface area of this figure?

[   ]

Do you UNDERSTAND?

3. Writing Explain how you found your answer to Exercise 2.

_____

_____

_____

4. Error Analysis What error was made in calculating the surface area of the square pyramid? Calculate the correct surface area.

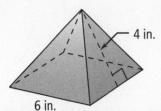

- 4 in.
- 6 in.

$$4\left[\tfrac{1}{2}(6)(4)\right] = 4(12) = 48 \text{ in.}^2$$

_____

_____

_____

Volumes of Rectangular Prisms

Common Core State Standards: 6.G.2: Find the volume of a right rectangular prism … by packing it with unit cubes … show that the volume is the same as would be found by multiplying the edge lengths of the prism. Apply … $V = lwh$ and $V = bh$ to find volumes of right rectangular prisms … .

Launch

City park workers plan to dig a rectangular hole for a small fishpond.

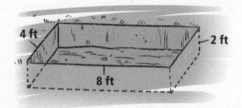
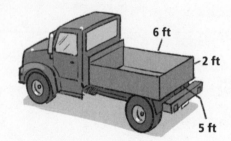

Will they be able to haul away the dirt in one truckload? Justify your reasoning.

Reflect

Suppose the dimensions of the hole were 4 ft long, 2 ft wide, and 8 ft deep. Would the hole hold the same amount of dirt? Explain.

_____

_____

_____

_____

Close and Check

Focus Question

You use nets to find the surface area of a box. How do you figure out how much fits in a box?

_____

_____

_____

Do you know HOW?

1. How many $\frac{1}{2}$ in. by $\frac{1}{2}$ in. by $\frac{1}{2}$ in. cubes does it take to fill the box below?

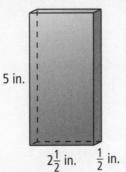

5 in.

$2\frac{1}{2}$ in. $\frac{1}{2}$ in.

2. What is the volume of the prism below?

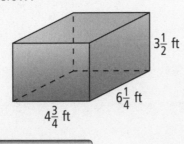

$3\frac{1}{2}$ ft

$6\frac{1}{4}$ ft

$4\frac{3}{4}$ ft

Do you UNDERSTAND?

3. Reasoning Will 500 ft^3 of gravel fit inside a container that measures $7\frac{1}{4}$ ft by $15\frac{3}{4}$ ft by $4\frac{3}{4}$ ft? Explain.

_____

_____

_____

_____

_____

4. Writing How many $\frac{1}{3}$ cm by $\frac{1}{3}$ cm by $\frac{1}{3}$ cm cubes will fit in a 1 cm by 1 cm by 1 cm box? Explain how you know.

_____

_____

_____

_____

_____

_____

_____

Problem Solving

Common Core State Standards: **6.G.2:** Find the volume of a right rectangular prism ... solving real-world and mathematical problems. **6.G.4:** Represent three-dimensional figures using nets ... and use the nets to find the surface area ... solving real-world and mathematical problems.

Launch

The toy company offers a robotic dog condo made of wood with openings for a square window and a square entrance.

Draw a net for the dog condo.

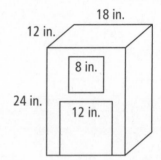

Then find the surface area of the condo.

Reflect

Could you draw more than one correct net for the dog condo? Explain.

_____

_____

_____

Close and Check

Focus Question
What can knowing the surface area and volume of 3-D figures allow you to do?

_____

_____

_____

_____

Do you know HOW?

1. Find the surface area and volume of each figure. Then circle the figure that has the greatest surface area and the least volume.

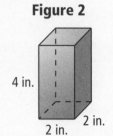

Figure 1

1 in.

4 in.

4 in.

4 in.

Figure 2

4 in.

2 in.

2 in.

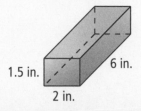

Figure 3

1.5 in.

6 in.

2 in.

	Surface area	Volume
Figure 1		
Figure 2		
Figure 3		

Do you UNDERSTAND?

2. Reasoning Using an 8-inch by 10-inch sheet of paper, is it possible to build a rectangular prism with a length of 5 in., a width of 4 in., and a volume of 60 in.^{3}? Explain.

_____

_____

_____

_____

_____

3. Writing Is it possible for two solids to have the same volume, but different surface areas? Tell when this would be helpful to know.

_____

_____

_____

_____

_____

Statistical Questions

Common Core State Standards: 6.SP.1: Recognize a statistical question as one that anticipates variability in the data related to the question and accounts for it in the answers. **6.SP.5.b:** ... Describing the nature of the attribute under investigation ... .

Launch

Sort these questions into two categories. Then describe your categories.

| How long does it take students to get to school? | What is your favorite color? | Did the cafeteria serve pizza today? |

| How many books do students read each month? | What fruits do students like to eat? |

Category 1 Questions	Category 2 Questions

Description	Description

Reflect

Will some of the questions provide more useful information than others? Explain.

_____

_____

_____

_____

Close and Check

Focus Question

How can a question have more than one answer? How do you decide which answer to use?

_____

_____

_____

Do you know HOW?

1. Fill in the chart with Y or N to identify whether the question is statistical.

Question	Statistical Question? Y or N
How long do students spend on homework each night?	
How tall are you?	
How many students in your class rode the bus to school today?	
What is your favorite season?	

2. Read the statements about statistical questions. Put an X in the box next to statements that are correct.
A statistical question...

☐ has more than one answer.

☐ will always have the same answer.

☐ is used to collect data about an aspect of the world.

Do you UNDERSTAND?

3. **Vocabulary** Is _"What is the high temperature each day this month?"_ a statistical question? Explain.

_____

_____

_____

4. **Reasoning** The data set shown answers the question _"How many eggs does a Blue Jay lay at one time (clutch size)?"_

4	4	5	3
3	5	4	5
5	3	4	7
4	2	3	4

What can you conclude about the average clutch size of a Blue Jay?

_____

_____

_____

_____

Dot Plots

Common Core State Standards: 6.SP.4: Display numerical data in plots on a number line, including dot plots ... . 6.SP.5: Summarize numerical data sets in relation to their context. 6.SP.5.c: ... Describing any overall pattern and any striking deviations from the overall pattern ... .

Launch

A principal is deciding how many computers to order for a new lab. Each classroom has submitted a vote. Show the data in a better way to help the principal make a decision. Tell why your way is better.

Computers for New Lab

Room 101 - 10	Room 201 - 4
Room 102 - 10	Room 202 - 10
Room 103 - 8	Room 203 - 8
Room 104 - 4	Room 204 - 8
Room 105 - 20	Room 205 - 10
Room 106 - 2	Room 206 - 8

My Way

Why It's Better

Reflect

Is there one right way to display data? Are some ways better than others?

_____

_____

_____

_____

Close and Check

Focus Question

What kinds of information can a dot plot easily show you? In what types of situations might you want that information?

_____

_____

_____

_____

Do you know HOW?

1. Your class keeps track of the number of hours they spend on homework each week. Display the data in the dot plot below.

10, 7, 5, 4, 5, 8, 10, 4, 6, 6,
5, 7, 4, 7, 5, 4, 5, 7, 8, 8, 6

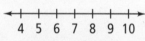
4 5 6 7 8 9 10
Number of Hours

2. What is the most frequent amount of time spent on homework?

[   ] hours

3. How many students spend 6 hours on homework each week?

[   ] students

Do you UNDERSTAND?

4. Vocabulary What is the difference between a cluster and a gap?

_____

_____

_____

_____

5. Error Analysis The dot plot shows the scores on a recent math quiz. A classmate states that only 7 students took the quiz. Explain the error, and tell how many students took the quiz.

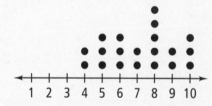
1 2 3 4 5 6 7 8 9 10

_____

_____

_____

_____

Histograms

Common Core State Standards: 6.SP.4: Display numerical data in plots on a number line, including …
histograms … . **6.SP.5:** Summarize numerical data sets in relation to their context.
6.SP.5.c: … Describing any overall pattern and any striking deviations from the overall pattern … .

Launch

A park worker writes out ticket sales information for his boss.

18 tickets from 10 A.M. to noon

24 tickets from noon to 2 P.M.

56 tickets from 2 P.M. to 4 P.M.

62 tickets from 4 P.M. to 6 P.M.

24 tickets from 6 P.M. to 8 P.M.

What is a better way to show the sales data?

Reflect

Why is your way to show the ticket sales better?

_____

_____

_____

Close and Check

Do you know HOW?

1. Use the resting heart rate data in beats per minute (bpm) to complete the histogram.

Resting Heart Rate						
86	72	92	83	91	84	86
71	66	93	87	89	81	98

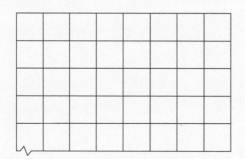

2. Use the histogram from Exercise 1 to complete the following statements.

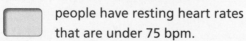 people have a resting heart rate between 80 and 85 bpm.

people have resting heart rates that are under 75 bpm.

Do you UNDERSTAND?

3. Reasoning A weather tracker records the temperatures for a week. Would a histogram be a good way to represent this data? Explain your reasoning.

Daily Temperatures (°F)						
74	73	76	76	74	75	75

_____

_____

_____

_____

4. Error Analysis Your classmate says that the histogram for Exercise 1 shows that most people have a resting heart rate between 85 and 90 beats per minute. Explain why he is not correct.

_____

_____

_____

_____

Box Plots

Common Core State Standards: 6.SP.4: Display numerical data in plots on a number line, including … box plots. **6.SP.5:** Summarize numerical data sets in relation to their context. **6.SP.5.c:** … Describing any overall pattern and any striking deviations from the overall pattern … .

Launch

A teacher sets up a kickball game by having students choose different whole numbers from 0 to 50. The student whose number ends up in the middle of all numbers chosen gets to be the referee.

Your classmates have already chosen the numbers shown. You get to go last in choosing numbers. Can you be the referee? Explain.

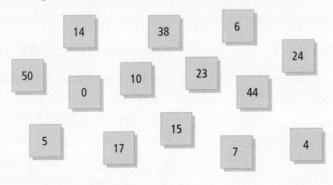

Reflect Were there any students you knew could not be the referee based on their numbers? Explain.

_____

_____

_____

_____

Close and Check

> ## Focus Question
>
> What kinds of information can a box plot easily show you? In what types of situations might you want that information?
>
> _____
>
> _____
>
> _____
>
> _____

Do you know HOW?

1. People at the local store were surveyed about their wait time. Find the boundary points and create a box plot. Waiting times in minutes: 5, 10, 6, 14, 3, 2, 15, 12, 11

Wait Time

0 1 2 3 4 5 6 7 8 9 10 11 12 13 14 15 16

minutes

Minimum: [   ]   Middle of Data Set: [   ]   Maximum: [   ]

Middle of the Lower Half: [   ]   Middle of the Upper Half: [   ]

Do you UNDERSTAND?

2. **Reasoning** Your uncle waited for 3 minutes. Did he wait more or less than the most of the others? Explain.

_____

_____

3. **Error Analysis** The scores **86, 77, 45, 19, 53, 75, 62, 20, 42, 89, 100** are displayed in class. Your classmate says that 50% of the scores are above 75. Explain the error, and correct the statement.

_____

_____

Choosing an Appropriate Display

Common Core State Standards: 6.SP.4: Display numerical data in plots on a number line, including dot plots, histograms, and box plots.

Launch

Your soccer coach posts results of ticket sales for a team fundraiser for new uniforms. You are the player who sells 94 tickets.

Uniform Fundraiser
Tickets Sold

44, 59, 66, 73, 74, 76
80, 83, 88, 91, 94

Make a dot plot, histogram, or box plot to display the sales data.

Then tell why you chose the type of graph you made.

Reflect You chose one of three types of graphs to display the data. Which of the other two graph types did you like the least for the data and why?

_____

_____

_____

_____

Close and Check

> ## Focus Question
> Which data displays are more useful in which situations?
>
> _____
>
> _____
>
> _____
>
> _____

▶ Do you know HOW?

1. Circle the data display that can help you answer the question, _How many students scored exactly 80% on the test?_

dot plot   histogram   box plot

2. Write a T for true or an F for false next to each statement.

☐ A histogram is helpful to see each data value.

☐ A dot plot is helpful to see frequencies of data values.

☐ A box plot is helpful to see clusters and gaps in data values.

☐ A histogram is helpful to see large data sets in data values.

3. A graph shows the total number of inches of precipitation that falls each month. It does not show daily totals. Is the graph a dot plot, a histogram, or a box plot?

☐

▶ Do you UNDERSTAND?

4. Reasoning A soccer coach keeps track of the goals made during the season. He wants to compare the number of goals made by each player. Should he display the data as a dot plot or histogram? Explain.

_____

_____

_____

_____

5. Compare and Contrast How are dot plots and histograms similar? How are they different?

_____

_____

_____

_____

_____

_____

_____

Problem Solving

Common Core State Standards: 6.SP.4: Display numerical data in plots on a number line, including dot plots, histograms, and box plots. **6.SP.5.a:** Reporting the number of observations.

Launch

A marketing team asked executives how many gigabytes of storage their music players should contain. They used a box plot to describe the responses and chose the middle value, 6 gigabytes, as the preferred storage space for the player.

Gigabytes for Music Player

1, 4, 4, 8, 6, 8,
7, 4, 10, 8, 4

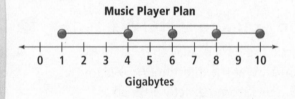

Do you agree with the marketers' thinking? Tell why or why not.

Reflect Does it matter what graph you choose when showing data? Explain.

_____

_____

_____

_____

Close and Check

Do you know HOW?

1. The dot plot below shows the number of runs scored for each baseball game. Place an X next to the statements that correctly describe the data.

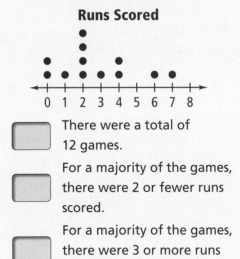

Runs Scored

☐ There were a total of 12 games.

☐ For a majority of the games, there were 2 or fewer runs scored.

☐ For a majority of the games, there were 3 or more runs scored.

2. Your friend bought 5 songs. Did she buy more or less than most of the others?

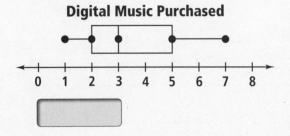

Digital Music Purchased

Do you UNDERSTAND?

3. **Reasoning** A customer service representative receives ratings from the people he helps. Scores above 6 are considered good. He makes this histogram to show his ratings. Is it misleading? Explain.

Customer Service Scores

_____

_____

_____

_____

_____

Median

Common Core State Standards: 6.SP.3: Recognize that a measure of center for a numerical data set summarizes all of its values with a single number . . . . **6.SP.4:** Display numerical data in . . . box plots. **6.SP.5:** Summarize numerical data sets in relation to their context, such as by: **6.SP.5.c:** Giving . . . median . . . .

Launch

Before building a new version of the video game "Zombie Pretzel Attack 2!", you survey gamers on the ideal number of characters Version 3 should have.

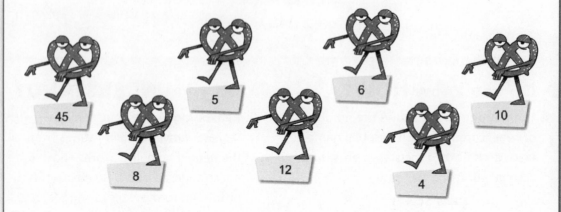

45   5   6   10   8   12   4

Based on the data, how many characters should you have in "Zombie Pretzel Attack 3!"? Explain.

Reflect

How did the result "45" affect your thinking about choosing the number of characters? Explain.

_____

_____

_____

_____

Close and Check

Focus Question

How can you represent a collection of numbers using just one number? How is using one number helpful? How is using one number *not* helpful?

_____

_____

_____

_____

Do you know HOW?

1. What is the median of the data set?

137, −150, 55, 17, −101, 179

2. You measure the height of people in your family and record the results in inches.

41.5, 67.2, 63.4, 64,
46.1, 72.4, 43.7, 57.8

Fill in the correct values to complete the box plot.

Family Member Heights (in.)

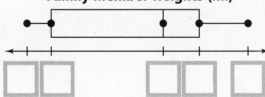

Do you UNDERSTAND?

3. Reasoning In Exercise 2, is the median an appropriate measure of center for the data? Explain.

_____

_____

_____

_____

_____

4. Error Analysis A classmate records the gasoline prices on the way to school.

$2.60, $2.79, $2.82, $2.67, $2.70

He says the median of the data set is $2.82. Explain the error your classmate made and find the correct median.

_____

_____

_____

_____

_____

16-2 Mean

Common Core State Standards: **6.SP.3:** Recognize that a measure of center for a numerical data set summarizes all of its values with a single number... . **6.SP.5:** Summarize numerical data sets in relation to their context, such as by: **6.SP.5.c:** Giving ... mean... .

Launch

Five friends set out with their packs for a long hike. After a while, the trailing hiker yells out, "This just isn't fair!"

What do you think the hiker means? Find a way to make the situation fair.

Reflect

Could you have made it fair by having everyone carry the median amount of weight shown?

_____

_____

_____

_____

Close and Check

Focus Question

You've learned about the median of a collection of numbers. How can you represent a collection of numbers using a different number? How do you choose which number to use?

_____

_____

_____

_____

Do you know HOW?

1. What is the mean of the data set?

37, 50, 53, 17, 10, 49

2. Your teacher says the mean of your test scores is 87. You have kept a record of all your test scores except one. What is the value of your missing test score?

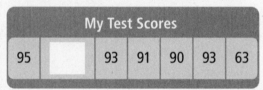

My Test Scores						
95		93	91	90	93	63

3. Your teacher says you may drop your lowest score if it raises the mean. What would be the new mean of your test scores?

Do you UNDERSTAND?

4. Vocabulary Your classmate describes the data below by using a measure of center, 21.5.

25, 4, 78, 18, 7, 63

Explain how you know which measure of center he used.

_____

_____

_____

_____

5. Reasoning Did your classmate use the appropriate measure of center to best describe the data? Explain.

_____

_____

_____

_____

_____

Variability

Common Core State Standards: 6.SP.2: Understand that a set of data ... has a distribution which can be described by its ... spread ... . **6.SP.3:** Recognize that ... a measure of variation describes how its values vary with a single number. Also, **6.SP.5, 6.SP.5.c.**

Launch

While developing a new sports drink, you ask members of two groups how many sports drinks they buy each month.

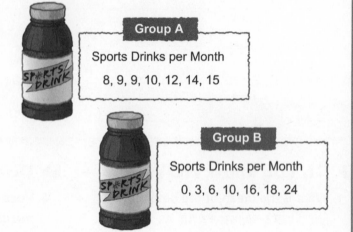

Group A

Sports Drinks per Month

8, 9, 9, 10, 12, 14, 15

Group B

Sports Drinks per Month

0, 3, 6, 10, 16, 18, 24

Use the data. Give at least one way the groups are alike and one way they are different. Which group would you like to have test your new drink? Why?

Reflect

Suppose you knew only the mean number of drinks purchased by each group per month. Would you choose a different group to test your drink? Explain.

_____

_____

_____

Close and Check

> ## Focus Question
> You know how to represent the middle of a collection of numbers. What else do you
> need to understand a data set?
>
> _____
>
> _____
>
> _____

Do you know HOW?

1. Look at each graph. Label the
variability as low, high, or none. Then
find the range.

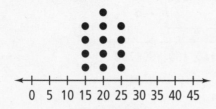

variability: [＿＿＿＿]

range: [＿＿]

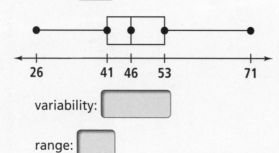

variability: [＿＿＿＿]

range: [＿＿]

Do you UNDERSTAND?

2. Writing A veterinarian records the
weight of the pets she sees in her
office. Describe the data set, including
measures of center and variability.

Weight of Pets (pounds)			
40.8	15.9	2.7	52.8
23	7	48.5	36
0.3	63.2	6	14.6

_____

_____

_____

_____

3. Reasoning If the maximum value is
ignored, does the variability change?
Explain.

_____

_____

_____

_____

Interquartile Range

Common Core State Standards: 6.SP.3: Recognize that … a measure of variation describes how its values vary with a single number. **6.SP.5:** Summarize numerical data sets in relation to their context, such as by: **6.SP.5.c:** Giving … variability (interquartile range …) … .

Launch

Which race was more competitive, this year's or last year's?

This Year's Car Race

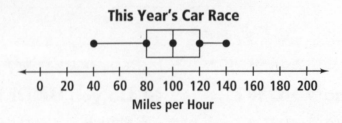

Last Year's Car Race

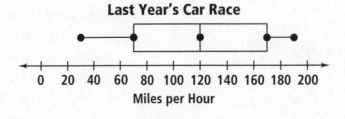

Tell how you know, and provide a possible reason for the difference in race results.

Reflect

Suppose you knew only the median speed of each race. Could you tell which race was more competitive?

_____

_____

_____

Close and Check

Focus Question

How can you represent the variability of a collection of numbers with one number? Why would you want to?

_____

_____

_____

_____

Do you know HOW?

1. The drama club records the total number of tickets sold for each performance. Find the interquartile range (IQR) for the given data set.

Number of Tickets Sold

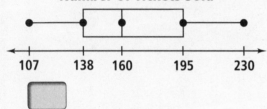

107   138   160   195   230

☐

2. The summer reading program records the number of books that each participant reads. Use the data to complete the table.

32, 16, 43, 10, 44, 31, 48, 6
19, 27, 39, 21, 11, 25, 8, 36

Books Read over Summer Break			
Median		First Quartile	
Minimum		Third Quartile	
Maximum		Interquartile Range	

Do you UNDERSTAND?

3. Reasoning What does the IQR tell you about the variability of the following data set?

Monthly High Temperatures (°F)

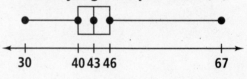

30   40 43 46   67

_____

_____

_____

_____

4. Writing Explain how IQR and variability are related.

_____

_____

_____

_____

_____

Mean Absolute Deviation

Common Core State Standards: 6.SP.5: Summarize numerical data sets in relation to their context, such as by: **6.SP.5.c:** Giving ... variability (... mean absolute deviation) ... describing ... any striking deviations from the overall pattern .... Also, **6.SP.3.**

Launch

A coffee shop wants to serve coffee at the same temperature every time for best taste. On average, both shop workers hit the shop goal. But the shop manager thinks one worker does a better job than the other.

Coffee Temperature by Cup (°F)							
Worker A	155	160	150	145	170	175	165
Worker B	155	160	163	157	162	158	165

· ·

Tell what temperature the shop wants the coffee to be. Then explain who the manager thinks did a better job.

Reflect

Can you think of another example of when you want something done just right and not too much or too little?

_____

_____

_____

_____

Close and Check

> ## Focus Question
>
> You've learned about the interquartile range of a collection of numbers. How can you represent the variability of a collection of numbers using a different number? How do you choose which number to use?
>
> _____
>
> _____
>
> _____
>
> _____
>
> _____

▶ Do you know **HOW?**

1. The mean of a data set is 5. The minimum of the data is 2. What is the deviation of the minimum?

Use the graph for Exercises 2 and 3.

Age of Skateboarders at Park

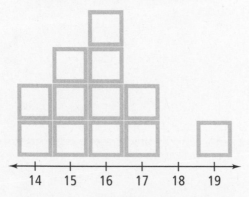

14	15	16	17	18	19

2. The mean of the data is 16. Fill in the absolute deviation for each data point.

3. What is the mean absolute deviation (MAD) of the data?

▶ Do you **UNDERSTAND?**

4. Compare and Contrast How is the deviation of a data value the same as and different from the absolute deviation of that data value?

_____

_____

_____

_____

5. Reasoning If the mean is a better measure of center for a given data set, does the MAD or interquartile range (IQR) better represent the variability? Explain.

_____

_____

_____

_____

Problem Solving

Common Core State Standards: 6.SP.5: Summarize numerical data sets in relation to their context, such as by: 6.SP.5.d: Relating the choice of measures of center and variability to the shape of the data distribution and the context in which the data were gathered. Also, 6.SP.3.

Launch

You are the coach of the girls' basketball team. Two of your players each claim to be the star player on the team.

Use at least one statistical concept – median, mean, variability, or mean absolute deviation – to compare the players. Describe the qualities of each player and decide which player is the team's star.

Points Per Game

Player A	Player B
28, 8, 11, 4, 33, 2, 40	16, 19, 14, 18, 20, 17, 22

Reflect

Suppose it's the eighth game of the season. Do you have the information you need to decide who should take the last shot? If not, what else would you want to know?

_____

_____

_____

_____

Close and Check

Focus Question

How can you use measures of center and variability to make decisions?

_____

_____

_____

_____

Do you know HOW?

1. You perform a science experiment that measures plant growth. You give only water to the control group. You give a special fertilizer to the variable group. You measure the heights of the plants in each group after 2 weeks.

Plant Heights (centimeters)

control group			variable group		
4	4.2	3.6	7.3	3.4	3.8
3.8	4.3	4.5	6.7	6.9	3.6
3.6	3.3	4.7	6.8	6.1	4.9

Use the mean of the plant heights to determine which set of plants grew taller.

_____

Use the mean absolute deviation (MAD) to determine which set of plants grew more consistently.

_____

Do you UNDERSTAND?

2. Writing The MAD of annual income is $12,000 for city A and $3,000 for city B. Explain whether this is enough information to decide where to seek employment.

_____

_____

_____

_____

_____

3. Reasoning Should Team A or Team B advance to the next competition? Justify your decision.

Long Jump Distances (meters)						
A	5.67	6.55	7.12	5.94	6.83	6.35	6.34
B	7.86	5.09	6.86	5.68	5.86	5.78	7.67

_____

_____

_____

_____

Formulas

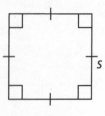

$P = 2b + 2h$

$A = bh$

Rectangle

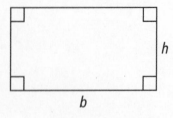

$P = 4s$

$A = s^2$

Square

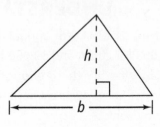

$A = \frac{1}{2}bh$

Triangle

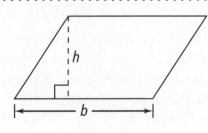

$A = bh$

Parallelogram

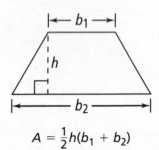

$A = \frac{1}{2}h(b_1 + b_2)$

Trapezoid

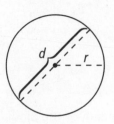

$C = 2\pi r$ or $C = \pi d$

$A = \pi r^2$

Circle

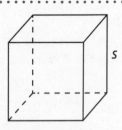

S.A. $= 6s^2$

$V = s^3$

Cube

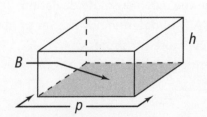

$V = Bh$

L.A. $= ph$

S.A. $=$ L.A. $+ 2B$

Rectangular Prism

Formulas

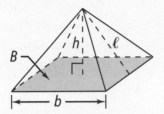

$V = \frac{1}{3}Bh$

L.A. $= 2b\ell$

S.A. $=$ L.A. $+ B$

Square Pyramid

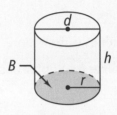

$V = Bh$

L.A. $= 2\pi rh$

S.A. $=$ L.A. $+ 2B$

Cylinder

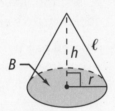

$V = \frac{1}{3}Bh$

L.A. $= \pi r\ell$

S.A. $=$ L.A. $+ B$

Cone

$V = \frac{4}{3}\pi r^3$

S.A. $= 4\pi r^2$

Sphere

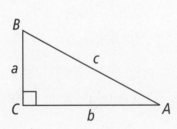

$a^2 + b^2 = c^2$

Pythagorean Theorem

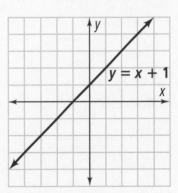

$y = mx + b$, where
$m =$ slope and
$b = y$-intercept

Equation of Line

Math Symbols

Symbol	Meaning		Symbol	Meaning
$+$	plus (addition)		r	radius
$-$	minus (subtraction)		S.A.	surface area
$\times$, $\cdot$	times (multiplication)		B	area of base
$\div$, $\overline{)}$, $\frac{a}{b}$	divide (division)		L.A.	lateral area
$=$	is equal to		ℓ	slant height
$<$	is less than		V	volume
$>$	is greater than		a^n	nth power of a
$\leq$	is less than or equal to		$\sqrt{x}$	nonnegative square root of x
$\geq$	is greater than or equal to		π	pi, an irrational number approximately equal to 3.14
$\neq$	is not equal to			
$(\ )$	parentheses for grouping		(a, b)	ordered pair with x-coordinate a and y-coordinate b
$[\ ]$	brackets for grouping			
$-a$	opposite of a		$\overline{AB}$	segment AB
$\dots$	and so on		A'	image of A, A prime
$^\circ$	degrees		$\triangle ABC$	triangle with vertices A, B, and C
$|a|$	absolute value of a			
$\stackrel{?}{=}, \stackrel{?}{<}, \stackrel{?}{>}$	Is the statement true?		$\rightarrow$	arrow notation
$\approx$	is approximately equal to		$a : b, \frac{a}{b}$	ratio of a to b
$\frac{b}{a}$	reciprocal of $\frac{a}{b}$		$\cong$	is congruent to
A	area		$\sim$	is similar to
ℓ	length		$\angle A$	angle with vertex A
w	width		AB	length of segment $\overline{AB}$
h	height		$\overrightarrow{AB}$	ray AB
d	distance		$\angle ABC$	angle formed by $\overrightarrow{BA}$ and $\overrightarrow{BC}$
r	rate		$m\angle ABC$	measure of angle ABC
t	time		$\perp$	is perpendicular to
P	perimeter		$\overleftrightarrow{AB}$	line AB
b	base length		$\parallel$	is parallel to
C	circumference		$\%$	percent
d	diameter		P (event)	probability of an event

Measures

Customary	Metric
Length	**Length**
1 foot (ft) = 12 inches (in.) 1 yard (yd) = 36 in. 1 yd = 3 ft 1 mile (mi) = 5,280 ft 1 mi = 1,760 yd	1 centimeter (cm) = 10 millimeters (mm) 1 meter (m) = 100 cm 1 kilometer (km) = 1,000 m 1 mm = 0.001 m
Area	**Area**
1 square foot (ft^2) = 144 square inches ($in.^2$) 1 square yard (yd^2) = 9 ft^2 1 square mile (mi^2) = 640 acres	1 square centimeter (cm^2) = 100 square millimeters (mm^2) 1 square meter (m^2) = 10,000 cm^2
Volume	**Volume**
1 cubic foot (ft^3) = 1,728 cubic inches ($in.^3$) 1 cubic yard (yd^3) = 27 ft^3	1 cubic centimeter (cm^3) = 1,000 cubic millimeters (mm^3) 1 cubic meter (m^3) = 1,000,000 cm^3
Mass	**Mass**
1 pound (lb) = 16 ounces (oz) 1 ton (t) = 2,000 lb	1 gram (g) = 1,000 milligrams (mg) 1 kilogram (kg) = 1,000 g
Capacity	**Capacity**
1 cup (c) = 8 fluid ounces (fl oz) 1 pint (pt) = 2 c 1 quart (qt) = 2 pt 1 gallon (gal) = 4 qt	1 liter (L) = 1,000 milliliters (mL) 1000 liters = 1 kiloliter (kL)

Customary Units and Metric Units	
Length	1 in. = 2.54 cm 1 mi ≈ 1.61 km 1 ft ≈ 0.3 m
Capacity	1 qt ≈ 0.94 L
Weight and Mass	1 oz ≈ 28.3 g 1 lb ≈ 0.45 kg

Properties

Unless otherwise stated, the variables a, b, c, m, and n used in these properties can be replaced with any number represented on a number line.

Identity Properties
Addition $n + 0 = n$ and $0 + n = n$
Multiplication $n \cdot 1 = n$ and $1 \cdot n = n$

Commutative Properties
Addition $a + b = b + a$
Multiplication $a \cdot b = b \cdot a$

Associative Properties
Addition $(a + b) + c = a + (b + c)$
Multiplication $(a \cdot b) \cdot c = a \cdot (b \cdot c)$

Inverse Properties
Addition
$a + (-a) = 0$ and $-a + a = 0$
Multiplication
$a \cdot \frac{1}{a} = 1$ and $\frac{1}{a} \cdot a = 1$, $(a \neq 0)$

Distributive Properties
$a(b + c) = ab + ac$ $(b + c)a = ba + ca$
$a(b - c) = ab - ac$ $(b - c)a = ba - ca$

Properties of Equality
Addition   If $a = b$,
             then $a + c = b + c$.
Subtraction If $a = b$,
             then $a - c = b - c$.
Multiplication If $a = b$,
             then $a \cdot c = b \cdot c$.
Division   If $a = b$, and $c \neq 0$,
             then $\frac{a}{c} = \frac{b}{c}$.
Substitution If $a = b$, then b can
             replace a in any
             expression.

Zero Property
$a \cdot 0 = 0$ and $0 \cdot a = 0$.

Properties of Inequality
Addition   If $a > b$,
             then $a + c > b + c$.
             If $a < b$,
             then $a + c < b + c$.
Subtraction If $a > b$,
             then $a - c > b - c$.
             If $a < b$,
             then $a - c < b - c$.
Multiplication
If $a > b$ and $c > 0$, then $ac > bc$.
If $a < b$ and $c > 0$, then $ac < bc$.
If $a > b$ and $c < 0$, then $ac < bc$.
If $a < b$ and $c < 0$, then $ac > bc$.
Division
If $a > b$ and $c > 0$, then $\frac{a}{c} > \frac{b}{c}$.
If $a < b$ and $c > 0$, then $\frac{a}{c} < \frac{b}{c}$.
If $a > b$ and $c < 0$, then $\frac{a}{c} < \frac{b}{c}$.
If $a < b$ and $c < 0$, then $\frac{a}{c} > \frac{b}{c}$.

Properties of Exponents
For any nonzero number n and any integers m and n:

Zero Exponent $a^0 = 1$
Negative Exponent $a^{-n} = \frac{1}{a^n}$
Product of Powers $a^m \cdot a^n = a^{m+n}$
Power of a Product $(ab)^n = a^n b^n$
Quotient of Powers $\frac{a^m}{a^n} = a^{m-n}$
Power of a Quotient $\left(\frac{a}{b}\right)^n = \frac{a^n}{b^n}$
Power of a Power $(a^m)^n = a^{mn}$